Treasures of Grace

TREASURES OF GRACE
1

THE GIFT OF
PEACE

Kira Marie Mccullough and Keb Burns

WordCrafts Press

The Gift of Peace
Copyright © 2025
Kira Marie McCullough and Keb Burns

Hardback ISBN: 978-1-962218-70-2
Paperback ISBN: 978-1-962218-71-9

Cover concept and design by Mike Parker.

Published by WordCrafts Press
Cody, Wyoming 82414
www.wordcrafts.net

Contents

Introduction VII

Part 1
When You Want to Become the Best Version of You
All That and a Bag of Chips............................... 2
The Portrait Artist 7
Peas and Honey 12
The Price of Beauty.. 17

Part 2
When You are Dissatisfied with Your Life
Living in an Ugly Town 22
Cultivating Gratitude 29
The Real Thing 32
Mundane Magnificence 37

Part 3
When You are Struggling with Forgiveness
The Fog of War... 44
Truth and Tears.. 49
The Ultimate Debt 54

Part 4
When Disaster Strikes
Trees and Angels... 58
Tornado! 63
If the Time Comes 72

Part 5
When You are Anxious and Fearful
Plunging Under the Water 76
Pumpkin Seeds 81

PART 6
When Someone You Love Dies
WHEN YOU LOSE YOUR BEST FRIEND 88
THE WASHING MACHINE 94

PART 7
When You Find it Hard to Trust God
CAR TRIBULATIONS 102
LEARN WHAT'S NORMAL FIRST 107
THE MEEK SHALL INHERIT THE EARTH............................ 112

PART 8
When you are Suffering
A JOURNEY OF HOPE 120
ACROSS TIME AND SPACE 127
THE SHEPHERD OF MY HEART 130

PART 9
When You Want to Know God Better
THE THREE R'S 138
BEAUTIFUL STRANGER.. 145
AS THE WORLD TURNS UPSIDE DOWN.............................. 150
YOU STILL HAVE TO OBEY ME... 156

PART 10
When You Need a Miracle
GOD'S DREAMS ARE BIGGER 162
THE HIGHEST MOUNTAIN 170

INTRODUCTION

What does the Bible say about grace?

Scripture tells us that grace is a divine treasure. Both the Old and New Testament are full of allusions to precious commodities such as gems, pearls, gold, silver, aromatic perfumes and incense, rare herbs and spices, embroidered robes and fine linen. Bible verses are filled with mighty metaphors that cause our imagination to soar and bring joy to the heart:

- ❧ Fine linen is called the glory of the saints
- ❧ The people of God are compared to the precious gems in God's crown
- ❧ A virtuous woman is compared to a ruby
- ❧ The Kingdom of Heaven is called the pearl of great price
- ❧ Knowledge is more precious than gold
- ❧ Wisdom is better than jewels

The writers of Scripture make it obvious that these material treasures are metaphors for spiritual riches, bestowed freely by the Father on his children. These are treasures of God's favor, treasures of grace.

Yet, the bible also tells us of treasures that one can see, touch, and experience, such as the breastplate of Aaron studded with twelve varied precious gems, or the Ark of the Covenant or the golden candlesticks of the Jewish Tabernacle. Through our eyes of faith, we believe that the walls of the Heavenly Jerusalem will be bejeweled with every kind of valuable stone, with gates fashioned of pearl and streets paved with gold. Through grace we receive the faith to believe in these amazing verses.

The analogies and metaphors of grace are abundant and rich

in the bible. Yet, grace has a more literal meaning, as well. Grace is one of those concepts that is hard to put into words. It is defined in many different ways:

- free and unmerited favor
- the life of God in the soul
- bestowed virtue
- help in time of struggle, perhaps unsought
- approval, pardon, privilege
- sanctification, reprieve, regeneration, and more

Though these are facets of the diamond called grace, all agree on the most brilliant of its attributes, its most defined and clear definition:

Grace is a gift from God, freely bestowed out of love, which enables the soul to become more like God.

We cannot merit or earn it, as symbolized in the story of the Prodigal Son in the Bible, when the son offered to be a servant in his father's house but was refused. Instead, he was received back as a son. We cannot earn the treasures of grace, because we are not paid servants in the Lord's house; we are sons and daughters. But we can ask for it. In fact, we should ask for it. We need it.

Grace makes easy that which is difficult by nature. Faults we find impossible to overcome on our own power can be overcome by the gift of God's grace. We have only to ask, accept, and put into practice.

...but he said to me, "My grace is sufficient for you, for power is made perfect in weakness." I will rather boast most gladly of my weaknesses, in order that the power of Christ may dwell with me.

~2 Corinthians 12:9

What does the Bible have to Say about Peace?

You and I know that we live in terribly troubled times, perhaps worse than the days of Noah and the Flood. We are beset by trials, faced with the shrinking value of our income and the increasing cost of living; shaken by wars and rumors of wars; anxious about plagues, and fearful of famines. If ever there was a time in history when mankind needed peace, it is now.

Peace is one of the treasures of grace bestowed on us when we first dedicate ourselves to God. Many people speak of the feeling of deep peace that fills them when they turn their lives over to Christ. But somewhere along the way, troubles and hardships erode the soil and sap the strength of the nascent flower called peace. Rattled by the terrors we see in the world and shaken by the sorrows in our own lives, we let go—bit by bit—of our union with God and thus our serenity. Like the Prodigal Son, we squander the riches of grace given to us by the Father until we have nothing left.

Fortunately, the Father is waiting for us to return so that he may once again bestow upon us the riches of his household—the grace we desperately need and the crown jewel of peace. In your hand, you hold a map for the road home.

How to use this Book

These one-day sessions are perfect for a month-long study, and include personal experiences that will inspire you in your spiritual growth and help you in your prayer life. However, this book lends itself to any situation or time frame, so feel free to pick it up and read any passage whenever you are in need of comfort, inspiration, or encouragement.

If studying daily for thirty days, set aside a block of quiet time to read the essay and scripture passage. Then spend a little time talking to God in your own words. The first step on the road is prayer. Through this book, you will practice how to pray with the honesty and trust of a child. When a child needs his mother or runs to his father, he comes just as he is—with scraped knees, runny nose, and tears streaming down his face.

Since we all know which road is paved with unfulfilled good intentions, it is important to turn good thoughts into good actions. At the end of each session, you'll find a suggestion for one very small but very practical action you can take to implement the grace you asked for. Think of this grace-in-action as one little pearl or bead of precious gemstone. After all, what's the point of asking for a gift if you never unwrap it?

At the end of thirty days you will have a string of thirty beads of costly gems, pearls, gold, and silver for your treasure chest in Heaven, freely given by a loving Father.

> *Do not store up for yourselves treasures on earth, where moth and decay destroy, and thieves break in and steal. But store up treasures in heaven, where neither moth nor decay destroys, nor thieves break in and steal. For where your treasure is, there also will your heart be.*
> ~Matthew 6:19–21

PART 1

When You Want to Become the Best Version of You
Creating Peace Through Self-Transformation

ALL THAT AND A BAG OF CHIPS
Making Peace by Developing Virtue
by Kira Marie McCullough

I'm overcoming the vice of gluttony, which means that I am learning to avoid mindlessly eating bowls of popcorn or plates of chocolate brownies while I'm watching reruns of *The Andy Griffith Show*. The key word is *learning*. If you invite me to your house for a party, please do not put a large container of potato chips in front of me. And definitely do not include a variety of cheesy-beanie-guacamole side dips. If you do, there may be nothing left but a few salty crumbles and half-eaten dips for the rest of your guests.

My children will tell you that when they were growing up, my gluttonous eating habits were an embarrassment to them. They would chastise me, pleading for portion control by saying, "Mom, pour some in a *small* bowl," hoping their intervention would prevent me from experiencing an artery-clogging medical emergency. Sometimes, they even hid the super-sized party bags of potato chips beneath piles of laundry or at the back of a dark closet.

For many years I have been a connoisseur of salty snacks, which I love almost as much as sweets (should I add that it is just as dangerous to put a plate of gooey fudge or oatmeal cookies within reach?). However, my children had grown and flown the nest before I realized that my problem was not potato chips, chocolate brownies, pizza, or rhubarb pie. Rather, I suffered from something much more serious.

The day of discovery occurred while I was automatically stuffing my mouth with apple slices and goat cheese. A healthy snack,

2

right? I was feeling rather satisfied with my food choice until I experienced an unexpected and brilliant illumination of conscience. Unlike the Apostle Paul, I wasn't riding a horse when the Lord spoke to me, but I was riding the thin line between a virtue and a vice. Suddenly, with surprise and guilt, I became aware that I was eating and eating and eating—*without being hungry*. In fact, I felt rather bloated and full. Yet, I continued munching fruit and cheese. The truth dawned on me—eating without being hungry had become a habit so ingrained that I had never realized it until that very moment.

Over the next several days, I prayed and tried to understand the source of this bad habit. This led to another epiphany: Overeating my favorite foods had become a way of dealing with overwhelming stress. If I felt depressed, insecure, or anxious, I would turn to the pantry or the fridge. This seemed a fair trade, and a more benign habit than drinking a six-pack of beer or binge-watching my favorite TV shows (neither of which, fortunately, has ever been a temptation for me).

It was humbling to admit that I had been flirting with the vice of *gluttony*. In fact, I have to admit with chagrin that it was worse than flirtation—gluttony and I were seriously dating.

We might be tempted to attach this vice to those with extended bellies and oversized clothing. However, in my case, gluttony was never obvious, for I am a small-boned woman who has mostly maintained a proper weight. Perhaps that is one reason this vice escaped my notice for so many years.

You may be asking, what is the definition of *vice*? It is the tendency to reach for the forbidden fruit of a pleasure that is taken to an extreme. Eating tasty food is enjoyable. Regularly eating too much is a vice.

Vices often begin with a tiny sin that turns into a lifelong habit. When our passions and desires become disordered, we seek the good in what is forbidden, just as Adam and Eve were tempted to eat the fruit from the tree of the knowledge of good and evil.

The woman saw that the tree was good for food and pleasing to the eyes, and the tree was desirable for gaining wisdom. So she took some of its fruit and ate it; and she also gave some to her husband, who was with her, and he ate it.
~Genesis 3:6

Sin offers us a temporary happiness that eventually pops like a balloon, exploding into regret. Adam and Eve's choice to eat the forbidden fruit turned into original sin, which has infected all of mankind since the dawn of time. But God had a better plan. He sent his Son, Jesus, to show us how to overcome our vices and live holy lives of joy and peace. Instead of bringing us a long list of *do nots* he made a short checklist of *do's*.

"Teacher, which commandment in the law is the greatest?" He said to him, "You shall love the Lord, your God, with all your heart, with all your soul, and with all your mind. This is the greatest and the first commandment. The second is like it: You shall love your neighbor as yourself. The whole law and the prophets depend on these two commandments."
~Matthew 22:36–40

We are designed by our Creator to love what is good, beginning with God himself, and then we are called to love our neighbor. Love is at the heart of the kingdom of God. The obstacle is our tendency to meet our deepest needs for love in ways that are sinful.

The funny thing is, we are all easily deceived into believing that the sinful choice we make is a "good one." We want to subdue our anxieties and experience peace, so we choose to overeat, or complain, or gossip, unaware that the temporary pleasure of indulging our flesh comes at a price. Like the serpent slithering through the Garden of Eden, there is a seductive temptation at work within the shadows of our vices. We want God's peace—which is a good desire—but we want it *our way*. Gluttony was my way. However, indulging in salty or sweet snacks resulted in a *faux* peace.

This is why vices become habitual, because we crave the feeling of *all is right with the world*, even if fleeting.

But there is something more to be desired, if we will ask for it, and that is the peace of God, *his way*. Such a peace is certain as the sunrise and lasts much longer than a gallon of tutti-frutti ice-cream.

> *In contrast, the fruit of the Spirit is love, joy, peace, patience, kindness, generosity, faithfulness, gentleness, self-control. Against such there is no law..*
>
> ~Galatians 5:22, 23

Once we have tasted God's peace, there isn't any vice that will suffice. Still, it can be a battle. Even after recognizing my tendency towards gluttony, I had to resist. I had to acknowledge the temptation immediately, and like a cowboy herding a maverick cow, cut it off at the pass. I made it a practice to stay away from the snack aisle in the grocery store, a near occasion of sin if there ever was one. Pass by the potato chip bowl at the party. Listen to my body when it says, "I am full."

Gluttony tempted me to make food an idol. Virtue invites me to grow in moderation and temperance. Every day, I am learning to exercise self-control over my selfish appetites so that I might freely choose what is healthy and good for both body and soul.

Temptations abound, and often the ones we fall for are those least apparent to our conscious minds. They are easier to see when we understand that vices serve as poor substitutes for the real thing—the genuine peace in our hearts, souls, and minds—which only God can give.

> *Peace I leave with you; my peace I give to you. Not as*

the world gives do I give it to you. Do not let your hearts be troubled or afraid.

~John 14:27

Storing Up Treasures in Heaven

Do you struggle with a specific temptation? Is there one particular vice that seems to easily entangle you? Consider that every vice has an opposite virtue. Pride is a vice that is countered by humility; anger is subdued by patience; lust is conquered through purity. Meditate on the virtue that is opposite your besetting vice and ask the Lord to help you grow in righteousness. Ask God for the grace to desire that virtue, and for the fortitude and persistence to pursue the good, the lovely, and the pure. In a Bible concordance, find scripture verses that mention the virtue, and memorize at least one passage. Find a friend who can be your prayer partner and confidante on the journey. Seek the help of a pastor, priest, or counselor if necessary. Overcoming vices can be challenging, but God will give you the grace to say "no" to every temptation. He will replace your vice with a virtue that will make you happy, healthy, and holy. Don't give up. You can do it!

But the fruit of the Spirit is love, joy, peace, patience, kindness, goodness, faithfulness, gentleness, and self-control; against such things there is no law.

~Galatians 5:22, 23

THE PORTRAIT ARTIST
Creating Peace Around Us

by Keb Burns

I am an artist, and my artwork looks like me.

I was a teenager when I began to sell my work at local art shows. The shows were fun, and I was always thrilled when a customer liked my work enough to actually pay money for it. It gave me a great deal of joy to paint it and made me happy when someone else found joy in it, too.

However, one thing puzzled me. Often, someone would look at the figures in my paintings and say, "They look like you." How could that be? They clearly weren't me; they were just figures from my imagination or portraits of other people. I mentioned this to my parents, who were also artists and my first art teachers. At the dinner table one evening I asked, "Why do people say my paintings look like me?" My father glanced at my mother with a knowing smile.

"Because they do look like you," my mother answered.

She explained that it's a common trait of artists to unconsciously paint themselves into their portraits. They also put their personalities into other kinds of art as well: landscape, still-life, sculpture, even abstract. That bothered me. A portrait should look like the subject, not the artist.

"This must be a characteristic of amateurs," I said, with a touch of disdain. My mother shrugged. "I don't think we can help it," she replied. I wasn't convinced. Real artists don't do that, I was sure! I concluded that I needed to study art under an experienced professional to get rid of this bad habit.

At an art show one weekend, I discovered two outstanding portrait artists with many years of experience and excellent reputations in portraiture. Both of these women taught classes, and I decided to choose one and ask if I might be allowed to become a student. But which one? Each had a slightly different style.

Wandering back and forth between their booths, I saw that each artist had made portraits of famous people to show they could paint an accurate likeness. Both had done portraits of the actor John Wayne, and both likenesses were excellent. And yet they were different. The John Wayne in the first booth looked down on the crowd with a kindly twinkle in his eye. The John Wayne in the second sneered at us with a steely-eyed stare. Both were clearly John Wayne, just John Wayne with two different personalities. Then I noticed that all the portraits in the first booth had soft, smiling, gentle expressions and all the portraits in the second had hard, cynical faces.

I decided to interview each artist to see which would be the better teacher. The first artist was a kindly, gentle woman who talked about her love of art. She told me about her wonderful husband, her angelic grandchildren, her love for the Lord, and how she enjoyed playing the organ at church on Sunday.

The second artist spent most of our interview talking about her rat of an ex-husband and how he cheated on her, cheated her out of all her money in the divorce, and turned her ungrateful adult children against her. She went on to complain about dishonest gallery owners (who cheated her), the organizers of the art show (who cheated her), and stupid, rude customers (who cheated her). I looked up at her portraits, hanging all around me. The faces glared down at me as if they thought I was going to cheat her, too.

I suddenly realized I was witnessing the phenomenon my mother was talking about. These two artists painted excellent, accurate likenesses of their subjects, but they somehow painted their own feelings and personalities into the images. These were not the right teachers for me.

Since neither of these two artists could teach me how to

avoid this fault, I thought perhaps I could learn better from the great masters. I decided to go to the library (no internet in those days) and check out every book on every famous portrait artist I could find. Perhaps by studying their works I could learn how to overcome this flaw. The revelation came with the first books I took home. On page after page, the paintings all reflected in some way the life of the artist. The coffee table edition of the collected works of Rembrandt struck me the most.

Rembrandt painted a vast collection of works over his lifetime: historical and mythological scenes, allegories, Biblical characters, portraits of civic leaders, and more. The truth hit me as I saw Rembrandt's soft, doe-like eyes looking out from every face, whether it was his own self-portrait, the Head of Christ, or the father of the Prodigal Son. Even the faces of animals! His sketch of a resting lion has the same eyes and expression as his self-portraits.

That's when I began to understand this phenomenon. It's not a flaw. We don't put ourselves into our work because we are amateurs; we put ourselves into our work because we are artists. The expression of self is the essence of the creative instinct. Creation is the visible manifestation of the invisible "Me." Manifesting our thoughts and feelings is the artist's raison d'etre. While we can sometimes suppress the trait by following a disciplined formula, such as in commercial or technical art, we can't hide it when we are creating something for the pure joy of creating.

When you look at a work of art in a museum, you are looking at a material object that was once an immaterial thought in someone's mind. This is quite an extraordinary thing, when you think about it, that we can take invisible thoughts and feelings and create a physical object that radiates those same thoughts and feelings to the viewer.

I found this fascinating. How do we do this? How do we glop our feelings and personalities onto a paintbrush and spread our souls all over a piece of stretched linen cloth? I am many decades older now, and I still don't know how we do it.

The ancient Greeks were likewise fascinated by this phenomenon of how thought and feeling can be turned into physical matter. They gave this phenomenon a name. They called it "logos", a force of creative thought so strong, it could manifest visibly as a physical thing.

The Apostle John brilliantly used this logos concept to introduce Christ into Greek culture. In the first lines of his Gospel, John explained that the creative thought behind the existence of all things was not an impersonal cosmic force but a Divine Person, the Second Person of the Trinity. "In the beginning was the Logos, and the Logos was with God and the Logos was God..."

Unfortunately, there is no exact translation in English for the word logos. It has traditionally been translated into English as "word", but this is far short of its rich meaning. Whenever I read the first Chapter of John, I like to read it this way:

"In the beginning was the Divine Intellect, and the Divine Intellect was with God and the Divine Intellect was God...All things came to be through him and without him nothing came to be...and the Divine Intellect became flesh and made his dwelling among us."

Here, John tells us that the logos, the creative force of the Divine Intellect, is so powerful, not only did it turn God's invisible thoughts into material things like stars and trees and rocks and animals and water and people, the Divine Intellect Himself manifested as a visible, touchable, material man.

He is the image of the invisible God, the firstborn of all creation. For in him were created all things in heaven and on earth, the visible and the invisible, whether thrones or dominions or principalities or powers; all things were created through him and for him. He is before all things, and in him all things hold together.

~Colossians 1:15–17

10

So what does this have to do with the subject of peace?

Because we are made in his image, we have his characteristics. Just like God, we too impart our thoughts, feelings and personalities into what we create. And here is where this phenomenon gets a little scary. Human beings create more than just paintings and pottery. We create families, homes, workplaces, schools, communities and cities. We create tools and factories and machines and computers and software. We create books and magazines and websites and movies and music. We create civilization. Everything we create will visibly manifest what is going on inside us. We can't help it; it's in our nature. The state of the world around us is a picture of our souls. Is our world at peace?

Storing Up Treasures in Heaven

Looking Within:

As I begin this thirty-day devotional for peace of soul, I begin with an examination of conscience to look at what my past choices have created so far. I can see a picture of the current state of my soul by looking around me. Do I like what I see? What have I created so far on my piece of canvas, that part of my life that is under my control?

- Is my home in chaos or in order?
- Within my family, among my friends, have I created peace or war?
- Is my neighborhood, workplace, classroom a more beautiful place when I am there?
- Is my life a masterpiece in the making?

Prayer:

My Jesus, the wonderful thing about being an artist is that I can always start over if I don't like what I have created. Every morning is a fresh sheet of paper, an untouched white canvas. I ask you to completely fill my soul so that from now on, all my creations will not look like me anymore, they will look like you.

PEAS AND HONEY
Creating Peace with Others
by Kira Marie McCullough

When I was growing up, the graphic scenes of the Vietnam War appeared on our television set during the 10:00 news, long after I had gone to bed. In the evenings, my parents would listen as CBS anchor Walter Cronkite's dulcet voice announced another victory or defeat, alongside gruesome images of decimated buildings and slaughtered bodies.

In the 1960s, this was the first war to be broadcast on TV, rattling the sensibilities of the most staid. I was eight years old, and though my parents shielded me from the terrible images on the tube, they could not protect me from their own angst about the overseas conflict.

My father, a pastor and a man of peace, joined the anti-war movement, a nonviolent protest which included university professors and students, as well as the average concerned citizen. It was a respectable group. Mostly, they gave lectures at campus gatherings and wrote letters to politicians.

Although I was only a second grader, my father encouraged me to write a letter to President Nixon, asking him to stop the war. I was pleased to think that my father had such confidence in my persuasive writing abilities. So, with great seriousness, I got out a piece of paper and pencil, and in my childish scrawl and elementary spelling ability, I wrote:

"Dear President Nixon, please stop the war. Please bring more peas to the world."

Of course, I meant to write, "peace." My father found the

homonym swap so delightfully funny that he made a copy to send to the President, but kept the original for posterity's sake. I have often wondered if Mr. Nixon found the letter as amusing as my father had.

I remember that my mother joined the anti-war movement in the '60s, but in a much quieter, more delicate fashion. She did not carry placards in marches, nor give speeches at parades. She simply wore a golden necklace with a square pendant on which was engraved: *War is not healthy for children and other living things.*

The simple artwork and profound message captured my child-like imagination. Seeing my mother dress in a jeweled note with such confidence inspired me. I do not recall that my mother ever spoke of the Vietnam War; she let the locket do the talking. That silent protest—visible only in the art and words engraved on a golden square hanging from her neck—influenced me greatly. I decided that I would grow up to become a peacemaker—one who would always strive to protect children and animals from the scourges of combat.

One might say that my father and mother approached the Vietnam War from opposite perspectives. My father's direct manner of protest came in the form of a letter, sent to the greatest leader of the free world. It was a cry for peace that became an offer of peas. My mother's less overt protest came in the form of a necklace, visible only to a few. It was a cry for the future of our world, and it soothed like honey. Today, I am thankful for the unique ways that each of them showed their love for mankind. They mixed "peas" with "honey."

When my own parents were young, their mothers tried to make peas more palatable by mixing the green globules with a bit of honey. The imagery of making bitter vegetables sweet reminds me of the wisdom found in scripture, where we read that those who seek peace are most successful when they rein in their anger and control their tongues.

> *Pleasing words are a honeycomb, sweet to the taste and invigorating to the bones.*
>
> ~Proverbs 16:24

13

Our words have impact. Nevertheless, there is a big difference between winning a skirmish over peas with a toddler and winning the battle for peace on a worldwide scale. Jesus tells us in scripture that there will be wars and rumors of wars until the end of the age.

> *As he was sitting on the Mount of Olives, the disciples approached him privately and said, "Tell us, when will this happen, and what sign will there be of your coming, and of the end of the age?"*
> *Jesus said to them in reply, "See that no one deceives you. For many will come in my name, saying, 'I am the Messiah,' and they will deceive many.*
> ~Matthew 24:3–5

Jesus is explaining to his disciples—and to us, more than two thousand years later—that no human being has ever been able to manufacture everlasting peace, and nobody—regardless of their claims or appearance or strength of personality—ever will. Prime ministers and presidents may make promises that seem Christ-like, but perpetual peace and perfect justice for all—including the cessation of war throughout the earth—shall never be accomplished solely through persuasive words and human hands. Jesus continues:

> *You will hear of wars and reports of wars; see that you are not alarmed, for these things must happen, but it will not yet be the end. Nation will rise against nation, and kingdom against kingdom; there will be famines and earthquakes from place to place.*
> ~Matthew 24: 6, 7

Reading Jesus' words, we might ask ourselves: Shall we cower in bomb shelters and caverns, trembling with fatalism and fear? Absolutely not!

The Lord tells us that we should be aware of the signs of the times (wars, earthquakes, plagues, and famines) but without fear. That may seem impossible—but God likes to call us into the stormy seas, asking us to walk on water. When we trust him, keeping our eyes on Jesus, we keep our balance. His mighty hands steady us upon the Rock who is Jesus Christ, Himself:

"I have told you this so that you may not fall away."
~John 16:1

So what can you and I do to create peace in our own little sphere of influence? Although we cannot end world wars, we can resist the tiny conflicts that pop up in our day-to-day lives, whether it is a surly cashier or an offended friend lobbing rude comments. Minor irritations and spiteful encounters have a way of escalating into tensions between friends, family members, and others. To avoid this, we must be dedicated to our walk of peace with Christ.

"I have told you this so that you might have peace in me. In the world you will have trouble, but take courage, I have conquered the world."
~John 16:33

Jesus conquers through love. One day, we will see the fruit of his kingship flowering throughout the earth. But until then, we must seek a *peas and honey approach*—learning to speak the truth in love, whether out loud or with quiet actions. Only God will achieve everlasting worldwide peace, and his will be a victory through love, not domination, of hearts.

But a shoot shall sprout from the stump of Jesse,
and from his roots a bud shall blossom...
But he shall judge the poor with justice,
and decide fairly for the land's afflicted.
He shall strike the ruthless with the rod of his mouth,

and with the breath of his lips he shall slay the wicked.
~Isaiah 11: 1, 4

Storing Up Treasures in Heaven

It is possible, through prayer and persistence, to become *peas and honey* people. We cooperate with God each time we overcome the temptation to argue or attack others with insults. Instead, we win through sharing words of encouragement, life, hope, and truth. This is not easy. If *peas and honey* is a new habit for you, let others know that you are trying to change and ask them for their prayers and patience. Be willing to let them correct you when you fail. Seek the help of a counselor, pastor, or priest if necessary.

If *speaking* edifying words is difficult, try *writing* good words through texts and email. Compliment others for their talents, their virtues, or their kindness towards you.

If arguing is habitual with certain people, develop a few phrases that you can speak easily and quickly in tense conversations, such as, "That is interesting," or "Thank you for sharing that thought," or "I will have to think about that." Psychologists say that repeating, with composure, a phrase three times in answer to another person's rudeness will often shut down the debate. Regardless, do your best to disengage from arguments quickly, calmly, and peacefully.

Finally, pray the words of Ephesians 4:29, asking the Lord to help you grow in compassion and kindness towards others.

> *No foul language should come out of your mouths, but only such as is good for needed edification, that it may impart grace to those who hear.*
> *~Ephesians 4:29*

THE PRICE OF BEAUTY
A Peaceful Conscience

by Keb Burns

Christian Dior had no idea that he was making the life of a seven-year-old American girl miserable, but miserable I was. In the late 1950s, Dior's full, petticoated skirt designs had made the long journey from the runways of Paris down to the Sears Girls Department and into my little life. My mother fell in love with a particular brown plaid dress with a full Dior skirt and Peter Pan collar and bought it for me. Not only was this a color I despised, but the petticoat was made of a scratchy, stiff netting that was gathered around the waist into a raw, jagged edge. It always left me with an encircling rash. "Sit still! Stop scratching!" my mother would whisper threateningly as we sat in church. I couldn't wait to get that thing off as soon as we got home. When I complained to my mother about the petticoat she replied "That's the price of beauty, dear. Sometimes looking nice means being a little uncomfortable. If you think that's uncomfortable, try wearing high heels."

I had two dressy dresses, which my mother switched out on alternate Sundays. The other one was my favorite, a lovely cotton dress in shades of blue and turquoise. It was soft and comfortable too, so the price of beauty was pretty low in that one. I wanted to wear it every Sunday, but my mother insisted on rotating them so they would last longer.

We didn't have a washer or dryer in those days, so my mother washed my Sunday dresses by hand in the sink and hung them to dry over the kitchen stove. She would turn the gas burner on the lowest setting, and the ring of tiny blue flames would glow like a crown of teardrop sapphires, sending heat up into the gently billowing skirts.

There they were one Friday night, the brown dress I hated and the blue dress I loved, side by side, drying over the stove. I passed through our galley kitchen and joined my father in the adjacent den. It was my custom to sit with him as he watched the Friday Night Fights on TV and bombard him with silly questions, which he patiently answered. He would tell me about the boxers, explain their strategies, complain about the referee, and analyze the coaches' styles. I pretended to understand, and he pretended to believe I was interested, and we both enjoyed spending the time together.

We had been bantering like this for a while when something caught my eye in the kitchen. Looking through the doorway, I could see something orange and flickering reflected in the window over the sink. Curious, I went to the kitchen door and looked toward the stove, where my dresses were hanging. The hem of one was on fire. I turned to holler for my dad…but a thought came to me, and I closed my mouth. The dress that was on fire was the hated brown one. What a serendipitous bit of luck!

I calmly walked back to the couch and sat down. In the window, I watched the reflection of the flames climb the dress until they almost reached the collar. The whole kitchen was glowing with a bright, golden light. Certain that the dress was now beyond repair I finally spoke, "I think something is on fire!" My dad jerked his head around, saw the flames, jumped up and ran into the kitchen. By the time he got there, the flames were burning the paint off the vent hood and licking at the ceiling. I had no idea that fire could spread so fast. Now I was properly scared; I may have waited too long.

He turned off the burner, grabbed the dishpan, which had water in it, doused the dress and the vent hood, and pulled the remaining shreds of fabric down on the stovetop to smother the last of the flames with a pot lid. As he examined the sooty burn on the ceiling, my mother came running from the other end of the

THE PRICE OF BEAUTY

house, saw the smoking debris on the stove and wailed, "Oh no, not the brown one! I loved that dress!" My blue dress was unharmed.

"Good girl!" my dad said, "You saved us! If it hadn't been for you, the house might have burned down!" I suddenly felt terrible. I knew that *because* of me the house might have burned down. I started to tell him what I had done, but I couldn't bear to disappoint him after he had praised me. I also saw the genuine sorrow in my mother's face as she picked up the charred bits of fabric. I knew what she was thinking; her hard-earned money had just gone up in smoke.

The following Sunday my mom brought the blue dress to me to put on for church and said, "We can't afford to get you another dress right now, so you'll have to wear this one every Sunday." This is what I had wanted of course, but I wasn't happy about it. In fact, as I sat in the pew at church looking down at the pretty blue skirt, I realized that I didn't enjoy wearing it anymore. It felt like ill-gotten gains. The price of beauty had become too high for this dress. I may have looked beautiful on the outside, but I felt pretty ugly on the inside.

Storing Up Treasures in Heaven

Looking Within:

Nothing destroys inner peace like a guilty conscience. Whenever I am tempted to do something wrong to get something I want, I won't be getting it for free; I will be buying it with a very great treasure: peace of soul. As I go through my day today, I will keep my heavenly treasure intact. I will choose a clear conscience over expedience.

Prayer:

My Jesus, please interrupt me when I get caught up in the heat of the moment, and remind me that peace is not a treasure I want to spend; it's a treasure I want to keep. Saying no to temptation is the price of beauty for my soul.

PART 2

When You are Dissatisfied with Your Life
Finding Peace in the Midst of Difficult Circumstances

LIVING IN AN UGLY TOWN
Making Peace with Where I Am
by Kira Marie McCullough

I was head over heels in love. Yes, in love with a house. Giddy with excitement, I could not wait for the day we would move into our quaint, one-hundred-year-old house in the Historic District, only a few blocks from the charming stores and brick streets of downtown. We had chosen to buy our home in an old-timey town, established in 1881 by a railroad mogul. Old-fashioned buildings stood sentinel around the city square, and the original red-brick streets meandered from the center of downtown into a variety of residential streets. These picturesque neighborhoods grew into a lush oasis of beauty in what would eventually evolve into an ugly town.

We called our home *the pink house* for its salmon color. The wide veranda welcomed us for sweet tea in the summer and beckoned us for hot cider in autumn, while indoors the original hardwood floors gleamed golden-brown, expelling the fragrance of seasoned wood.

In the beginning, our lives were rather peaceful, wrapped up in the happy duties of my husband's job with a nearby church, and my responsibilities of caring for our family. As a piano teacher and stay at home mother, I spent most of my days either indoors or puttering about the glorious landscape of our little *Garden of Eden*.

Ancient oaks lined the road where we lived, and generations of mourning doves nested in the wide sheltering branches, glorifying God with a morning chorus and evening hymn. This was a cheerful place, surrounded by the external symmetry of flower beds and shaded by crepe myrtle and ash trees. Lush stands of bamboo bounded our property, and creeping vines trellised the fenceposts. I used to brag that every window featured a breathtaking view. Yet, we were only minutes from the more modern version of our city, with its traffic, gas stations, and impoverished districts.

Three years after purchasing our home, we experienced extreme hardships that led to many changes in our lives, including foreclosure. The dream of Eden had been shattered by forces more powerful than I, and we lost our pink house. We were cast out into new realms of our city.

We moved first to a duplex on the southside. A tiny square of grass and one lone tree had replaced our front yard with its syca-mores and wildflowers. The only views from our bedrooms were of fences dividing us from our neighbors. Cooing mourning doves vanished, superseded by squawking black-feathered grackles. But worse than that, we had been transplanted to a new subdivision linked by a network of busy streets directing traffic to shops, malls, and restaurants. I could see an intersection of stoplights from my front door.

In my dream-state of living in the pink house, I had not noticed the major changes happening in my town. In an effort to lure big business and more residents, the city fathers had voted for the expansion of freeways, development of subdivisions, and erection of new strip malls. Farmland, fertile with corn and okra and sorghum, disappeared almost overnight. Bulldozers mowed down old growth forests to make way for apartment complexes and filled winding creeks with concrete for parking lots. It seemed that every square inch of the city had been sold to someone, and everyone preferred brick and mortar to trees and fields.

They say that beauty is in the eye of the beholder; however, I think that there is an objective form of beauty that almost every-one can see in the glories of Creation. My standard for natural beauty had been set during my childhood years, growing up in the foothills of the Appalachian Mountains. The splendor around me had sparked creativity, helping me develop my skills as a writer. As a child gazing out the window or sitting beneath the silver-leafed olive trees, I took my observations to pen and paper, describing everything around me.

Today, I still thrive on natural landscapes and beautiful views. I am inspired by walks on wooded trails, the sound of birdsong, the colors of creation. Yet, when cast out of my private garden-life, I lost my inspiration. I entered into a desert of discontent.

Over the next decade, we would move several times, renting apartments and houses, always within earshot of the humming noises of the city. I admit, I tried to flee the metropolis—more than once. Every year, I plotted to go somewhere else in Texas—Taylor, Horseshoe Bay, Kerrville—anywhere but here. However, my plans were consistently dashed by financial woes, job issues, or other considerations.

At the time of this writing, I have dwelled in this concrete and cement city for almost fifteen years—longer than anywhere else that I have lived over my six-plus decades of life. It has not become a prettier place.

Strangely, though, I have become more content. I have accepted my situation. Finding peace with where I am has enlarged my capacity to live fully in the moment, enjoying my life despite the garishness of manmade surroundings. It was a challenging process, getting to this point. But looking back, I realize there were four key pillars to my personal transformation.

Discover Snapshots of Beauty in the Mundane

Notably absent from my terrain are panoramic vistas of purple mountains and green valleys fed by meandering crystal rivers. Instead, a hodge podge of unpleasant buildings, highways, and rushing cars greets me daily. However, if I look closely at the small stuff around me, I will find snapshots of beauty everywhere. On a mile-long strip of grass where I take my daily walks, there are tiny things that make me happy. I delight in the clusters of Mexican heather with lavender blooms, and the lazy bumblebees humming between the flowers; the drooping branches of the juniper tree that cover me like an umbrella as I stroll beneath it; a burst of yellow beyond the fence posts, signifying the wild cinquefoil victorious over the weeds. God's goodness can be found in unusual places, and the splendor of creation is waiting to be discovered in the midst of the busy city, if only I will train my eyes to seek the tiniest pleasures, the smallest of delights.

Count my Blessings

Thankfulness is a guaranteed mood changer for me. Lately, I have been counting my blessings while taking my walk along the strip of grass that stretches the length of the road by my apartment. My goal is to think of fifty blessings by the end of my exercise routine. I am often amazed by what comes to my mind—from the simple enjoyment of a hot cup of coffee or clean sheets on the bed, to the enormously important godsends, such as family, friends, and church. I have made *counting my blessings* a regular activity, based on my meditation on 1 Thessalonians 5:18. This scripture tells us that gratefulness is God's will:

> *In all circumstances give thanks, for this is the will of God for you in Christ Jesus.*
>
> ~1 Thessalonians 5:18

Doing the will of God in the little things—like simply praising him for the tiny blessings found in an ugly city—pleases him. We sometimes think we can only please God in big matters, like becoming a missionary to faraway countries or heeding the call to become an evangelist to the urban slums. These are marvelous ideas; However, we can also please him by simply saying often, and from the heart, "thank you."

Grow in Patience

Have you heard the saying, "Don't pray for patience—you'll get it"? This is often spoken tongue in cheek, because we all know that in our human weakness and selfish tendencies, we are prone to be impatient—rash, hasty, anxious, angry, and proud. We want our way, and we want it now. In my ennui about living in an ugly town, I would occasionally become frustrated enough to send a flurry of resumes to employers in pretty places, like Virginia or upstate New York. In these moments, my mind was not focused on rational considerations (such as the cost of moving, or how I would really feel about leaving my family in Texas). Rather, strong emotions and unruly passions churned inside, and I listened to these. Thankfully, I did not get my way. This wrestling match with frustration sparked my initial lessons in patience. I discovered that patience is a virtue *not* to be avoided. It is the key to finding peace in every uncomfortable circumstance. Saint Teresa of Avila concurs:

> *Let nothing disturb you,*
> *Let nothing frighten you,*
> *All things are passing away:*
> *God never changes.*
> *Patience obtains all things*
> *Whoever has God lacks nothing;*
> *God alone suffices.*

The virtue of patience has increased in my soul through prayer. When I pray for patience, I find tranquility springing like a bubbling fountain in my heart and mind, fed by the tributary called fortitude. This gift of fortitude strengthens us to withstand our adversities and troubles; overcome our hastiness and sadness; and quench our selfish desires. Fortitude is the courage to persist, while patience is the happy waiting for what we hope for. In this happy place of the soul, we do not fret about the answers to our prayers,

26

for we know that God, in his wisdom, power, and love, will provide what we need, when we need it. Both patience and fortitude are virtues acquired through prayer and effort. God's grace bestows virtues upon us when we ask, but we must activate his gifts by making daily choices to be patient and persistent.

Offer the Prayer of Relinquishment

This is a powerful devotion, not to be taken lightly, for it is the total offering of what I desire most to God; I am abandoning my will to his. The prayer of relinquishment may require many days, even months—sometimes a lifetime—of repetition, as we slowly release our own desires and accept what God has given to us. This is what I have done with my longing to move somewhere else. When I finally gave up my yearning to live in a handsome house in a comely town or in a quaint countryside cottage, my discontent fled. I now have greater trust that God will guide me to the place that is best for me, even if that means staying in an ugly city.

Residing in an unattractive town is a small thing, a minor irritation. Yet, it is precisely these kinds of tiny, ongoing annoyances that can keep us from experiencing peace. Like a scratchy woolen sweater or pebbles in our shoes, we cannot think of anything else.

The answers that I have discovered may help you, too.

- Replace my grumbling with praise
- Uproot pride and grow in patience
- Relinquish my desires to God's will

Then, peace flourishes where there had once been a desert of discontent.

Storing Up Treasures in Heaven

Have past choices or unforeseen circumstances put you in a place that you do not like, but cannot seem to change? Perhaps you feel

27

stuck in a difficult relationship or dissatisfying job; maybe you feel trapped by financial woes or discouraged by living in an ugly city?

First, look for snapshots of beauty in the mundane. Find the tiny things in life that make you smile, in spite of your circumstances. As you pray for the patience to endure your trials, remember to count your blessings, thanking God for the simple things like a cup of coffee or clean sheets on the bed. Whatever your situation, bring your needs to God in prayer; honestly share your feelings, hopes, and fears. Take a moment to meditate on the scripture below, and then relinquish all of your troubles to God, asking him for the virtue of patience, the gift of fortitude, and the faith to trust that he has a good plan for your life.

> *For I know well the plans I have in mind for you—oracle of the Lord—plans for your welfare and not for woe, so as to give you a future of hope.*
>
> ~Jeremiah 29:11

CULTIVATING GRATITUDE
At Peace with Good Enough

by Keb Burns

As a landscape designer, I had been called to the home of a couple in an upscale neighborhood to create a design for their front yard. The wife greeted me graciously and showed me around their property, chatting animatedly about all of the different plants that were growing there. The husband remained silent as he followed us around.

The yard was beautiful. They had gracefully maturing trees and shrubs, flowering annuals, and a lush, green lawn. Everything was well-designed, neatly trimmed and fertilized. I was puzzled about why they had called me, because their yard was already such a showplace. Frankly, I wasn't sure how I could improve on it. When I asked them how I could help them, the wife pointed to the home across the street and said, "I want my yard to look exactly like that."

I turned to see the home she was pointing at. From the dark, fresh mulch, baby plants, and bright white limestone blocks that formed curving beds throughout the lawn I could see that this yard had been recently landscaped. Although I could tell that it had been done professionally, it wasn't done well. In fact, it was a little gaudy. Overkill is the word. The rustic limestone blocks were too big for the scale of the house and clashed with its classical style. The shrubs were the wrong choice for the climate, and the trees were too large a species to be planted that close to the driveway. Cracked pavement was in that family's future. There was a mish-mash of every kind of flower color in oddly shaped beds. I

29

had a feeling that at Christmas time, this was the house that was decorated with so many lights you had to put on sunglasses when you drove past it.

"But your yard is already so beautiful…" I said, trying to be diplomatic.

The husband spoke for the first time. "Yes, we had it done three years ago," he said glumly, "to look exactly like that yard". He pointed at the yard next door. It was done in the same style. The wife gave him a dismissive wave of the hand.

"Well, we can't be the last one in the neighborhood," she said, pointing at the rest of the block. I looked up and down the street and was surprised to see that the landscaper who had done the yard across the way had done the exact same design in several other yards, as well.

"That one was first," she said pointing at the farthest yard, "then that one, then that one…"

The neighbors were all copying each other.

"Why don't you just call the company that landscaped those yards? Why call me?"

"Because I want mine to look even better than theirs," she replied, "I want mine to be the best."

"What is this going to cost me?" The husband asked. I told him I would have to measure his property, and it would take me about a week to give him an accurate cost, but considering all of the limestone blocks, the pavers, the number of shrubs and trees, it would be in the thousands. He excused himself, asked his wife if he could speak to her in the house for a minute, and they stepped inside and closed the front door. I could hear muffled shouting, crying, and door slamming. I waited for a long while but finally realized that no one was coming back out, so I left. I never heard from them again.

This book is about maintaining peace of soul when trouble comes to visit. But sometimes we invent our own trouble deep inside our own hearts. Envy is a destructive nest of termites that eats away at our peace of mind from the inside out. Envy condemns us to the misery of perpetual poverty because no matter how much we acquire, we never have enough. It also condemns our loved ones to life with someone who is forever unhappy.

Theologians tell us that envy is a fault contrary to humility and charity because it causes us to resent the happiness of others. This is true but I think there is also another component to envy: ingratitude. Envy is also the inability to see the wonder and beauty we already have in our lives. Envy devalues every gift God gives us. It's as if every beautiful treasure God bestows on us crumbles into ashes as soon as it is placed in our hands. It's like having food that does not satisfy and water that does not quench.

This is one of the hardest vices to overcome and one of the most miserable to endure. For most people, it can only be overcome by the grace of God that comes from persevering prayer.

Storing Up Treasures in Heaven

Looking Within:

Fasting restores my sense of plenty and gratitude. I will set aside one day a week to fast from food, entertainment, outings, hobbies, shopping— anything I find that I am taking for granted or no longer feel grateful for.

Prayer:

My Jesus, I ask for the grace to be amazed today by the richness of everything I have. Fill me with the grace of gratitude and generosity. Let me know the joy of being happy for the good fortune of others while being overwhelmed and satisfied with the blessings you have bestowed on me.

THE REAL THING
Finding Peace Beyond this World
by Kira Marie McCullough

The fresh-faced young man wearing a green apron over his t-shirt and jeans bagged my groceries with gusto. Next, he rang up the total of my bill. "That will be $111.48," he said.

I smiled. Swiping my credit card, I reminisced, "Back in 1985, my husband and I could buy a week's worth of groceries for fifty bucks."

The cashier's eyes grew big as saucers, and his mouth dropped open with incredulity.

"Oh yes," I said, continuing my litany of prices from 1985, "A two-bedroom, one-bathroom house in Austin, Texas cost $400 monthly. We paid a car payment of fifty bucks, and pumped our tank with a twenty, since a gallon of gas hovered around a dollar. In 1985, a twenty could buy two Big Mac meals at McDonald's, a pair of movie tickets, and we would still have enough left over to purchase a bucket of popcorn and two sodas!"

"That sounds like Heaven!" the clerk said, gawking at me with awe and a smidgen of envy. I could see in his face a jealous longing to get into a time machine and travel back to what he thought were those good old days.

Putting my shopping items into the cart, I had a sudden inspiration. "Well," I blurted, "1985 might sound like a utopia compared to today's economy, but when it comes to Heaven, nothing can beat the real thing." As I walked away, I looked over my shoulder to see his surprise; he scratched his chin as if Heaven were a novel concept.

The encounter in the grocery store had a deeper meaning beyond a young man sharing the ennui of entrapment in 21st century inflation and a woman with one foot in the glorious '80s. Our conversation symbolized secret hopes for something better than our current situation. He wanted lower prices. I wanted to set his sights higher, catapulting him beyond the present troubles of our strained economy, launching his mind towards the true, the good, and the beautiful—*Heaven*.

Heaven is the real thing

Which reminds me of the 1971 advertising campaign by Coca-Cola. The popular TV commercial aired in living rooms across America, featuring a hundred youngsters on a hillside in Italy, crooning, "Coke—that's the real thing."

Apparently, Coke was not real enough, because a few years later, the company changed the recipe. In 1985, fierce competition with Pepsi-Cola drove the manufacturers to create a new formula called "New Coke." We tried it. Funny, it did not taste like Pepsi or Coke. Definitely sweeter than the original, but less sharp, sudsy and definitely less satisfying. New Coke sales tanked, and by 2002, the company had plucked the proprietary recipe from its dusty files and begun merrily making vats of the soda we had all known and loved, rebranding the original, calling it Coke Classic.

Sometimes, you just can't improve on the original.

How many of us today remember "New Coke" and its abject failure? We are so short-sighted that sometimes we forget there was a parody of the *real thing* called Coke. In a similar way, we are so earthly-minded that we sometimes forget that there is something that came before this ball of terra firma. Like the New Coke, the stuff of earth is only a shadow, a mirror image seen through a dim glass. The real thing is Heaven, and it cannot be beat.

To better understand God's plan for Earth and Heaven, we must begin at the beginning. First, there was God—the Father,

Son, and Holy Spirit, contentedly enjoying the circle of love flowing eternally between them. Desiring to share the abundance of love with creatures, the Triune God established the world and fashioned mankind, placing our first parents, Adam and Eve, in a lovely garden called Eden.

All was well, until sin entered the story. The serpent (the devil) presented an alluring temptation to Eve, who ate the forbidden fruit of the tree of the knowledge of good and evil. Adam, who stood nearby, ate what she offered to him, fully knowing their disobedience.

The result? They felt shame and went into hiding. God searched them out, and after a brief conversation, he acted swiftly with justice, first upon the evil one—

> *Then the Lord God said to the snake:*
> *Because you have done this, cursed are you among all the animals, tame or wild; On your belly you shall crawl, and dust you shall eat all the days of your life.*
>
> ~Genesis 3:14

There were consequences for Adam and Eve, as well. Cast out of the place of perfect fellowship with God and one-another, they left the garden, but with a promise:

> *I will put enmity between you and the woman, and between your offspring and hers; They will strike at your head, while you strike at their heel.*
>
> ~Genesis 3:15

This passage is considered by many theologians to be the protoevangelium—the first announcement of the Good News that God would send His Son, Jesus, as the Redeemer of mankind. Jesus' birth, death, and resurrection would triumph over the devil. The God-Man, Jesus, would undo the knot of original sin made by our first parents, and continued by our own actions.

To bruise the head of the infernal serpent, or devil, God would send the Savior in a human body, born of a woman. Scripture records that the Angel Gabriel was sent by God to Nazareth, to a virgin named Mary, who was betrothed to Joseph:

> *And coming to her, he said, "Hail, favored one! The Lord is with you." But she was greatly troubled at what was said and pondered what sort of greeting this might be. Then the angel said to her, "Do not be afraid, Mary, for you have found favor with God. Behold, you will conceive in your womb and bear a son, and you shall name him Jesus. He will be great and will be called Son of the Most High, and the Lord God will give him the throne of David his father, and he will rule over the house of Jacob forever, and of his kingdom there will be no end."*
>
> ~Luke 1:28–33

A never-ending Kingdom sounds too good to be true. On Earth, there is an end to everything. Nature's seasonal cycles bring demise to spring's flowers and winter's crushing snow splits trees; the most well-built homes eventually crumble beneath the weight of weather and time, and our bodies wither and waste away with age. All rulers, governments, and monarchies fade into oblivion, their conquests, riches, and fame relegated to the dusty tomes of history.

Only the Kingdom of God has no end, and yet, it has a beginning for each of us. It starts with our search for God, who made the Earth and everything in it. When we find God, we find joy.

The real thing is God's original plan of unbroken fellowship between us. Earth was made for man, but man was made for Heaven. The foretaste of Heaven is the sweetness of righteousness, peace, and joy that we can taste here and now, as the Kingdom of God reigns in our hearts, preparing us for an eternal future with God.

The penultimate real thing is God, Himself, who waits for us with open arms, if only we will trust Him with everything, if only we will welcome his Kingdom into our hearts, today and every day.

Storing Up Treasures in Heaven

When present times feel unbearable, and we carry burdens too heavy for our frail shoulders, we must focus on our eternal destination. Meditate on the scriptures below, imagining the incredible beauty and glory of our heavenly home, prepared for us by God from the beginning of time.

> *Rejoice and be glad, for your reward will be great in heaven. Thus they persecuted the prophets who were before you.*
>
> ~Matthew 5:12

> *But our citizenship[a] is in heaven, and from it we also await a savior, the Lord Jesus Christ. He will change our lowly body to conform with his glorified body by the power that enables him also to bring all things into subjection to himself.*
>
> ~Philippians 3:20, 21

> *But as it is written:*
> *"What eye has not seen, and ear has not heard, and what has not entered the human heart, what God has prepared for those who love him."*
>
> ~1 Corinthians 2:9

> *He will wipe every tear from their eyes, and there shall be no more death or mourning, wailing or pain, [for] the old order has passed away.*
>
> ~Revelation 21:4

MUNDANE MAGNIFICENCE
Peace in Ordinary Things
by Keb Burns

I was sitting at my mother's bedside at the nursing home, marking the long, drawn-out vigil of her slow decline. She was dying, but I wasn't sure whether or not she fully grasped that. The doctor explained it to her but in language cushioned by so much metaphor and euphemism, I wasn't sure she understood. She made no answer and didn't talk about it after he left.

I was knitting as she slept, trying to figure out the mysteries of a new pattern. It was turning into a long, quiet night. After a while, I checked my watch and then held up my knitting to see how far I had gotten. Suddenly, my mother said, "I remember sweeping the floor." I glanced at her and saw that her eyes were closed. She was talking in her sleep again. I went back to knitting.

"I remember mowing that big lawn with just a push mower."

"I remember folding the laundry."

"I remember trying to find meat. I had a ration card for it, but there wasn't any meat in the store. That was during the war, you know. I told you about rationing during the war, didn't I?"

I stopped knitting and looked at her. Her eyes were open, and she was looking at me. She wasn't talking in her sleep as I had thought; she was wide awake and talking to me.

"What are you talking about?" I asked.

"I was always angry about having to do all of those things. I thought it was a waste of time. All those chores kept getting in the way of real life. I wanted to be successful. I wanted to do important things. But I barely remember those important things now."

I suddenly realized that she had understood what the doctor told her; she was reviewing her life. She looked out the window and smiled. "I remember tying your shoes, and looking for a rubber band in the junk drawer so I could put your hair up in a ponytail. I remember helping my mother make potato salad. I remember trying to find a tie for your father's birthday in Dallas Cowboys colors. I remember when your older brothers had poison ivy at the same time. While I was putting calamine lotion on them, I dropped the bottle, and it spilled all over the bed, the floor, everywhere. What a mess. I remember taking your little brother to his school play. I remember riding horses with my father when I was a teenager."

She looked at the detritus on the bedside table, the crumpled tissues, the hand lotion, the empty pudding cup. She looked around the room at the laundry in the corner and my knitting bag on the floor. She pointed to all these things and looked at me earnestly. "See this? This is real life. Right here. Right now. You, sitting here with me now, and later when you go to the store, and then go home to wash your dishes." She sat up and leaned toward me to emphasize her words, as if she were telling me the location of a hidden treasure map with her last breath. "This is what life is made of. This is it!"

She laid back on the pillows and looked at the ceiling. Her voice trailed off as if she were talking to herself now. "And I missed it. No matter where I was, I was always restless because I wanted to be someplace better. No matter what I was doing, I was always resentful because I wanted to be doing something more important."

She whispered, "I wish I could go back."

My mother's life had its share of drama, but at the end, the cream that rose to the top in a rich layer of memory was the peace of doing simple things: dusting the blinds, sitting in the car reading while waiting for school to let out, wrapping Christmas presents with my dad at midnight on Christmas Eve, walking the dog, chatting with the family at the dinner table. And yet, she had not allowed that peace to enter her soul and dwell there. It was there for the taking; she just didn't take it.

"What would you do differently?" I asked.

"I wouldn't just sweep the floor; I would *enjoy* sweeping the floor."

On the way home that night, I thought about what she had said. When I got in, I picked up my Bible to find a passage that addressed my thoughts. After thumbing back and forth through the pages for a while, it struck me that the Scripture I needed was located right between Luke 2:52 and Luke 3:1. I call it, "Luke Chapter Two-and-a-Half." It's the silent book of the Bible, the one that covers all the years that Jesus, Mary, and Joseph lived an ordinary life in Nazareth doing ordinary things, so ordinary it wasn't recorded.

That God became man and lived a human life for thirty-three years on this earth is extraordinary enough. What's even more extraordinary is that only three of them were spent in active ministry. The other thirty years were spent doing what exactly? Sweeping, hauling water from the well, cutting wood, chatting around the dinner table, visiting with neighbors, eating, sleeping, feeding the donkey, shopping in the market stalls, repairing the roof, and a thousand other mundane things similar to what we do every day. Do the math: he spent 90.9 percent of his life on earth doing random, ordinary things. What was he waiting for, for heaven's sake? He had miracles to perform and sermons to preach and hypocrites to scold and people to raise from the dead! He had souls to save and a world to redeem! Why did he waste all that time?

He wasn't wasting time; he was using it well. While these were all ordinary tasks, this was no ordinary person sweeping the floor and mucking out the stable and chopping wood. This was a Divine Person doing these things and offering them all to the Eternal Father as a gift of love. And now, every sweeping of every floor, every mucking out of every stable, every bit of firewood that is ever chopped, is fixed permanently in the Eternal Father's mind and heart as a gift from his most beloved Son. Because of this, ordinary life is elevated and sanctified for the rest of us. After all, if the King himself steps down from his throne and sweeps the floor, could I dare say that sweeping the floor is beneath me? No, it has become a kingly task. And now, the Eternal Father sees Jesus' hand on my broom as I sweep.

Why did Jesus elevate these mundane things to such an exalted level? Because Jesus didn't come just to redeem our souls. He came to redeem our bodies, our work, words, actions, thoughts, feelings, recreation, relationships...*our whole lives*. He came to redeem creation itself and to restore to us the peaceful, intimate life we were all meant to have with him at the beginning of creation. This is the life Adam and Eve had when they walked and talked with God, face to face, in the Garden of Eden, when Heaven and Earth flowed together, without a veil between.

Sometimes, by focusing only on the last three years of Jesus' life, we miss the big picture. The big picture is this: Jesus came to restore the profound union of natural and supernatural that existed at the beginning of time. He began this restoration by deeply entering into our mundane lives and elevating the mundane to the magnificent. We invite that restoration into our lives by uniting ourselves to him in our everyday tasks. That restoration will be complete when Jesus comes again in glory.

As you go about your day doing ordinary things, make a conscious intention to unite your ordinary tasks to the ordinary, hidden life of Christ, and let the peace and joy of ordinary things enter your soul. Do as my mother said: don't just sweep the floor, *enjoy* sweeping the floor, because it is a kingly task, and across time and space, the King sweeps the floor alongside you.

Storing Up Treasures in Heaven

Looking Within:
While the ruby red Blood of Christ, shed for us on the cross,

is the crown jewel of the work of Redemption, there are also many other jewels of grace in the treasure chest of Christ's life. I want to turn the mundane tasks of my daily life into treasure, just as Jesus did.

Prayer:

My Jesus, I unite all of my tasks of this day to all of the ordinary tasks you performed during your hidden years in Nazareth. Offer my tasks to the Eternal Father along with your own. Let me work alongside you today for the salvation of souls.

PART 3

When You are Struggling with Forgiveness
Making Peace with God and Others

THE FOG OF WAR
At Peace with the Past

by Keb Burns

At the age of eleven my brother was already an expert on military strategy. He out-played the adult relatives at chess and strategy board games; he could explain all the major campaigns of the Civil War, in detail. He was a brilliant kid whose intellect made him a misfit among his classmates. In those days there were no talented and gifted programs. So, utterly bored and unchallenged at school, my brother poured his mental energy into all sorts of challenges that he devised for himself. One of them was the Living Room Wars.

At that time, my father was a struggling draftsman studying for his architectural license exams. With a wife and three kids there wasn't much money for luxuries such as furniture. The vast expanse of the living room, which spanned the width of the entire house, was empty except for carpet, mid-century modern wallpaper and venetian blinds. It was the perfect location to lay out every major battle of World War II.

My brother spent every dime of his allowance on big bags of plastic army men, a popular toy in the 1950s. He had collected, sorted, and categorized literally hundreds of plastic soldiers, artillery pieces, tanks, tents, ships, and planes. Each item was color-coded with a dot of model airplane paint to indicate the unit to which it belonged. With history books and maps spread out, he would set up these pieces wall-to-wall across the living room floor. Beginning with the starting position of all the units in major battles, he painstakingly moved each piece, one by one, according

44

to the historical accounts of real troop movements. When he finished playing out the battle as it occurred in history, he started over. Wondering what would have happened if General So-and-So had known this bit of intelligence, or if that unit had moved left instead of right, he played out alternative scenarios to see if the battle would have ended differently.

He was especially fascinated with how various combatants often had completely opposite views of how the battle was going. A letter home written by a sergeant might describe the battle as going well while a captain's diary would confide that they were losing. The truth of what was really going on was often obscured until a battle was long over. It was this confusion that he found fascinating. Would things have turned out differently had there not been that confusion? He would be engrossed in this project for days on end, which pleased my parents; it kept his restless intellect out of trouble. They gave me strict orders to stay out of the living room and leave my brother alone.

Of course, I didn't listen.

One day, bored with my dolls and curious about what other mischief I could get into, I wandered into the living room and asked, in typical four-year-old-fashion, "Can I play with you?"

My brother's face showed alarm as he watched my clumsy bare feet tip-toeing through the battlefield. He sighed, thought about it a moment, then said yes. He grabbed one of his bags of soldiers, dug through it and pulled out a plastic German Shepherd dog and a couple of soldiers.

"Here," he said, "you can be the K-9 Corps."

I was thrilled. Even my pre-school brain had enough sense to understand that I was bothering him. I had expected him to say, No! Go away! Instead, he kindly ordered Eisenhower and Runstedt to bring the Battle of the Bulge to a halt. So, for a little while, we played out a made-up battle where the heroic K-9 Corps bravely held off the German Army until finally, the courageous hero-dog, at the front of the action, took a bullet for the team and died. He was accorded full military honors and was buried on the battle-field. My brother even found a plastic soldier that was blowing a bugle. Placing it by the grave, he imitated the sad melody of "Taps" through pursed lips. It was quite moving.

At that, I was content to have played my small part in saving the world, and like any war veteran, relieved to go back to the peaceful world of domestic life. Because of the gap in our ages, we didn't spend much time together, so I was vastly satisfied that my brother had chosen to play with me. I felt loved.

The age gap between siblings often narrows as they become adults. Unfortunately, the distance between us enlarged as we grew older. After he returned from Viet Nam, he was more reserved than ever. He had seen things that he could never bring himself to talk about. War, it turns out, was not so glorious after all. His serious view of the world and my sheltered one didn't mesh. When we met on holidays, we had little to talk about. We loved each other, but we had become friendly strangers.

Years later, we found ourselves seated next to each other at a long string of tables in a Mexican restaurant during a family reunion. Our father had recently died, and, as is common at such times, we were all remembering our childhoods, reviewing our own lives, and thinking about our mortality. The effect of a few Margaritas had also loosened our tongues. My brother suddenly said to me, "I have a confession to make. You won't remember this, but I have felt terrible about it all these years. I have to get it off my chest."

He then recounted his memory of that afternoon when he stopped his war to play with me, only his version was different from the one I remembered. He told me he staged the death of the dog in order to get rid of me so that he could go back to his game. "It was mean, and it must have hurt your feelings. We didn't get to spend much time together, so I should have played with you as long as you wanted to play," he said. "I just wanted to tell you how sorry I am that I did that. It's been bothering me all these years."

Astonished, not only that he remembered it but at his view of it, I said, "I do remember it! You didn't do anything wrong; I did. Mom and Dad told me to leave you alone, and I knew I was bothering you, but you stopped and played with me anyway. And you played with me just long enough. After all, I was only four; I had a short attention span. You don't owe me an apology. You let me come into your world for a while, and I was happy. It's one of my all-time favorite memories."

It was his turn to be astonished at my view of the incident. He fell into a thoughtful silence. Then I saw his face relax and his shoulders slump as he leaned back against the chair. I could see a wave of peace visibly washing over him. He had put the burden down. After a while he mused, "It's funny how we can experience the same event but see it differently and make wrong assumptions about what's really happening."

"Yeah," I said. "Kind of like the fog of war, huh?"

He nodded yes. "If only people would talk to each other," he said.

We looked at each other sorrowfully. If only we had.

We all have regrets about things we have done that were wrong, things we have done that were good but badly done, and good things we should have done but didn't. This regret can rob us of all peace. But we must be careful and remember this admonition from Proverbs:

> *Trust in the Lord with all your heart,*
> *on your own intelligence do not rely;*
>
> *~Proverbs 3:5*

If we try to rely on our own frail memories, intellect, and judgement alone, we run the risk of falling either into the sin of presumption or the sin of despair. We may mistakenly presume that we are holy and in no need of repentance at all, or we may despair, thinking we are so horrible we can never be forgiven. The spiritual life is a battle, and we are easily confused by the fog of war. Do we really think our judgement is wiser than God's? He alone can judge us rightly.

Storing Up Treasures in Heaven

Looking Within:

When I review my behavior at the end of the day, I must neither make excuses for my misdeeds on the one hand or beat myself up in despair on the other. Both of these extremes are rooted in pride; I am too proud to be imperfect. Instead, I need only lay my failures down before the Lord, tell him I am sorry, and ask for the grace to turn away from sin and do better tomorrow. Just as important, I must not make judgements about others. I'm not walking in their shoes, and I don't see what God sees.

Prayer:

My Jesus, you know me better than I know myself. Let me see myself the way you see me so that I may know how much you love me but also the ways I can improve. I ask for the humility to face my sins honestly on the one hand but never despair of your mercy on the other.

TRUTH AND TEARS
Finding Peace Through Confession and Forgiveness
by Kira Marie McCullough

We stood in the middle of the parking lot, my friend and I, with a warm breeze whipping our hair and the sharp sun making us squint. The morning church service had ended, and most people had raced out of the parking lot in their cars, headed to Olive Garden or Cracker Barrel for lunch. We were less interested in food, and hungrier for the fellowship of our friendship. We had not seen one another in over a month.

Lingering beside our vehicles, we ignored the gusty air, the heat rising from the pavement, and the hot sun beating down upon our heads. We talked for an hour, shielding our faces with our hands, letting the wind unwind the curls from our hair. We exchanged memories from our past, some that made us laugh. But before long, we had both dredged up some of our most heartbreaking moments.

As my friend recalled a distressing time with her former husband—a period when he had verbally abused her—she began crying uncontrollably. Her tears dried quickly in the sun, becoming glittering lines down her cheeks. I reached out to hug her, and she sobbed on my shoulder.

Though many years had passed since that tragic time with her husband, the memories were fresh, and the wounds raw and real. Yet, in sharing the truth with me, she was relieved of a sorrowful burden that she had carried silently in her heart for far too long. This forged an even stronger bond between us, and proved the veracity of scripture:

A friend is a friend at all times, and a brother is born for the time of adversity.

~Proverbs 17:17

Confession opens the door of our hearts, inviting God's healing touch through the compassionate ministry of another person. For many of us, our closest confidantes are friends, brothers, sisters, mothers, or mentors. We may meet for coffee and chats, walks and talks, or stay up late at night typing texts or composing emails to one another. For others, rejuvenation is found in the quietude of a church confessional, where sins and failures are disclosed to a priest who reassures us of God's love and forgiveness.

In every truthful encounter and intimate friendship, there is an invisible Guest. The Good Shepherd, Jesus Christ, is in our midst, doing the inner work that makes us whole and complete.

The 23rd Psalm—the 24th Psalm in the New American Standard version—paints a pastoral picture of a Shepherd tending his flock of sheep. The poetic words act as a metaphor for God and his beloved children, whom he loves so much that he will search diligently for those who stray. The Prophet Isaiah tells us that the Good Shepherd is seeking his suffering, sickly, and lonely lambs. It is not the strong whom he carries, but the weak.

Like a shepherd he feeds his flock; in his arms he gathers the lambs, Carrying them in his bosom, leading the ewes with care.

~Isaiah 40:11

The world tells us to "grow up," "be strong," and to "make things happen." Our culture applauds and rewards the go-getters, the hard workers, the persistent entrepreneurs who carve a niche in the marketplace and put their name in the spotlight.

God's economy is different. It is not our confidence, but our human frailty that draws him, with tender compassion. He is wooed by our willingness to speak the truth about ourselves: *I am needy, I am weak, I don't know how to make it happen.*

When we admit that we are weary, he refreshes us. When we confess that we are wounded, he restores us.

> *He restores my soul. He guides me along right paths for the sake of his name.*
>
> ~Psalm 23:3

Like my friend, we often carry burdens of unforgiveness and of unhealed wounds for many years. Memories of past broken relationships or painful situations may cloud and darken our present moments. Allowing God to bring these recollections to our conscious minds—for the purpose of confession and forgiveness—is the first step towards renewed peace.

I remember a time of truth and tears in my own life, when I needed healing from the wounds received at the hands of a dear friend, an older woman, whom I revered and adored as if she were my own mother. We shared hot tea and cookies at her kitchen table, worshipped together at church, and spent hours talking on the phone. She had a marvelous sense of humor and a no-nonsense approach to solving problems. Our conversations were often punctuated by laughter as well as tears.

Over time, my friend surprised me by occasionally lobbing a snide remark, or snipping at me with a judgmental comment, leaving me confused. Though I dismissed the sporadic rudeness, this behavior increased, until one day, she said something egregious that changed my life. Her words were accompanied by actions that put me into a severe financial hardship. I could hardly fathom what had happened. The trust between us had been utterly broken.

Desperate for comfort and counsel, I called my sister on the phone. I felt like the little child who runs into the arms of her big sister after spending the day at school harassed by a bully. For over an hour, Deb listened as I shared everything that had happened. Then she offered this heartfelt advice:

> *Keep your eyes on the vision that God has given you; move forward; do not look back, and forgive the friend who betrayed you.*

That night, before going to sleep, I sat in bed and reviewed all of my offenses towards my friend. I thought of the Lord's Prayer, which Jesus taught us to say:

> *and forgive us our debts, as we forgive our debtors;*
> ~Matthew 6:12

As I admitted my anger to God, I could feel my brokenness consumed by His love. His gentle presence revealed that I should let go of my desire to judge her, leaving justice to God. The rest of the Lord's prayer came to my lips, and I forgave my friend. My prayer changed into praise, with happy thoughts fluttering like the pages of a book rustling in a breeze—words neither hurried or worried, but quiet, calm, and trusting. I was filled with joy in the company of God. My peace had returned.

> *Have no anxiety at all, but in everything, by prayer and petition, with thanksgiving, make your requests known to God. Then the peace of God that surpasses all understanding will guard your hearts and minds in Christ Jesus.*
> ~Philippians 4:6, 7

Truth has a way of setting us free from anxiety and restoring our tranquility. Truth reveals painful realities that offer us the opportunity to forgive others and find personal peace, even when relationships cannot be reconciled.

Tears have a way of cleansing the soul. Confiding our hurts to another can bring closure to past memories. Offering forgiveness in the privacy of prayer can heal our hearts.

No matter what has happened to you in previous years, if you will bring yourself into the light of God, allowing his grace to illuminate your mind, he will reveal the truth that will set you free, inspiring the tears that will release the pain and bring you peace.

And you will know the truth, and the truth will set you free.

~John 8:32

Storing Up Treasures in Heaven

Confession and forgiveness are best undertaken in the presence of another person. Set a time to meet with a trusted friend, counselor, pastor, or priest. Before your encounter, ask God to reveal any unresolved hurts or unhealed memories in your heart and mind. Take notes to share with your confidante. As you begin this journey of truth and tears, remember that the goal is to *let go* of the past so that you may live more gloriously in the present. Remember that God is your Good Shepherd, guiding you to an oasis of refreshment and renewal, where he offers you the most magnificent treasure of grace, the gift of peace.

If we confess our sins, He is faithful and righteous, so that He will forgive us our sins and cleanse us from all unrighteousness.

~1 John 1:9

The Ultimate Debt
Paying it Forward

by Keb Burns

A few years ago, I had a job working in the office of the church I attended, doing a variety of tasks. When you work for a church, you occasionally get assigned an unpleasant duty or two. One of the odd jobs that had somehow gotten stuck to me like a burr on my pant leg was that of bill collector. I was asked to collect on the overdue accounts for the ads on the back of the church bulletin.

One evening, we had a potluck supper for some special occasion, and it had attracted a goodly number of church members, most of whom were arriving in the parking lot at the same time I was. I noticed a few people who had overdue accounts, but this was not the time to talk to anyone about it, of course. However, that didn't matter to them. Word had gotten around that I was collecting, and my mere presence was enough to make them feel guilty. If you want to scatter a crowd in a hurry, put a bill collector in the middle of it. *Poor Matthew. He must have had a lonely life as a tax collector before he met Jesus,* I thought as I suddenly found myself all alone in the church parking lot.

Before Matthew met Jesus, he understood debt in a simple and brutal way. The Romans needed money, so they imposed a tax on the people, whether they could afford it or not. Matthew's job was to enforce Roman taxes, and he profited from it himself. For his wages he was allowed to add an additional tax for himself. If a person couldn't pay the tax, imprisonment was the penalty. Pay or be punished, that was the only system of debt that Matthew understood. That all changed the day Jesus invited himself to dinner at Matthew's house.

At dinner that night, Jesus made a simple statement that turned Matthew's view of debts and payments upside down. He said, "I desire mercy, not sacrifice." The Romans asked the people to sacrifice themselves to pay the Romans' debts. But Jesus spoke of a God who sacrificed himself to pay our debt for us! Matthew had never heard of such a thing! But then Jesus went one step farther. He asked us to have mercy on others as he had mercy on us. He asked us to pay this debt of love forward for our neighbors.

Is love a debt? Yes, it is. Jesus made that clear in the parable of the Unforgiving Servant, which must have made a big impression on Matthew because he remembered it and wrote it down later in his memoirs of his time with Jesus. You will find it in Matthew 18:21-35. In this parable, Jesus made it clear that forgiveness of neighbor isn't a take-it-or-leave-it proposition; it's the payment God requires of us in return for him paying our debt on the Cross. Like any debt, failure to pay will weigh on us heavily and rob us of our peace of soul. I can't explain it better than Matthew did himself.

> "But to you who hear I say, love your enemies, do good to those who hate you, bless those who curse you, pray for those who mistreat you. To the person who strikes you on one cheek, offer the other one as well, and from the person who takes your cloak, do not withhold even your tunic. Give to everyone who asks of you, and from the one who takes what is yours do not demand it back.
>
> Do to others as you would have them do to you. For if you love those who love you, what credit is that to you? Even sinners love those who love them. And if you do good to those who do good to you, what credit is that to you? Even sinners do the same. If you lend money to those from whom you expect repayment, what credit [is] that to you? Even sinners lend to sinners and get back the same amount.

But rather, love your enemies and do good to them, and lend expecting nothing back; then your reward will be great, and you will be children of the Most High, for he himself is kind to the ungrateful and the wicked. Be merciful, just as [also] your Father is merciful.

Stop judging and you will not be judged. Stop condemning and you will not be condemned. Forgive and you will be forgiven. Give and gifts will be given to you; a good measure, packed together, shaken down, and overflowing, will be poured into your lap. For the measure with which you measure will in return be measured out to you."

~Matthew 6:27–38

Storing Up Treasures in Heaven

Looking Within:

Giving, forgiving, and expecting nothing in return are all hard for me to do. And yet I expect others to do these things for me. Worse, I forget that God himself does this for me every time I offend him.

Prayer:

My Jesus, what you have asked of me is hard, even heroic. But I know that you would not ask the impossible. I need your grace to pay the debt of love forward to my neighbor. Bring to my mind someone who needs your love today.

PART 4

When Disaster Strikes
Finding Peace in Times of Trouble

TREES AND ANGELS
Peace During Crisis

by Keb Burns

On Sunday morning, August 17, 1969, Hurricane Camille was stalled just off the coast of Mississippi, sucking up power from the warm waters of the Gulf of Mexico like a boxer taking a deep breath before advancing on his opponent. My grandparents' little wooden-frame home was within sight of the beach, directly in the path of the storm's eastern eyewall, the part that packs the most punch. An emergency management team went through their neighborhood, knocking on doors to make sure everyone had evacuated. Every knock was met with a reassuring silence, meaning the residents had already gone.

When they came to my grandparents' house they were startled when my grandmother came to the door. She explained that her husband had decided to stay, though he was willing for her to evacuate without him. The team warned that this was going to be one of the biggest storms in history, and my grandparents would put their lives at risk if they stayed. "If he won't go," they told her, "you, at least, should get out." Grandmother replied that she would not leave without her husband. They had survived World War I, the Great Depression, and World War II together. If he was going to die, she was going to die with him.

My father and his siblings made multiple phone calls to their parents begging them to go before it was too late. Grandfather, who had grown deaf in his old age, could not hear my father on the phone. Nor could he hear the alarming reports on TV and radio. He was convinced that this storm would be no worse than the storms they had weathered in the past.

As the sun went down, Camille began to surge forward. When it became clear that nothing would convince them to leave, one of my cousins volunteered to stay with them. Abandoning his own evacuation plans, he made his way through the rising wind and rain to my grandparents' house and helped them prepare for the siege.

The three of them spent one of the most terrifying nights of their lives. Or rather, I should say, two of them did. My grandfather wasn't disturbed at all. While my grandmother and cousin could hear the screaming winds, breaking glass, splintering houses, boats crashing into buildings, and 300-year-old oaks ripping up out of the ground, my grandfather could hear nothing. He calmly read the paper and worked crossword puzzles by candlelight, sipped coffee, and dozed. My grandmother and cousin spent the night in prayer. Grandmother asked God to send angels to surround the house.

As the sun came up the next morning, the winds abated. My grandmother stepped out onto the porch to see what damage had been done. To her horror she saw that her neighbors' houses were gone. There was so much debris the streets were no longer visible. Miraculously, my grandparents' home was standing unscathed in this sea of unrecognizable rubble. All the ancient oaks in their yard had fallen in a protective square around the house, sheltering it from the wind, storm surge, and flying debris. The home was not visible at all through the leaves and branches, leading rescuers to think at first that the home was gone. The trees were resting so snugly against the walls of the house on all four sides, they had to climb over the trunks of the trees to get in the door. Other than a few missing shingles, the house was not even damaged.

We all go through storms of various kinds in life. Some storms are brief and mild, a mere inconvenience. Some are actually invigorating; we enjoy the challenge of overcoming them. Some storms, however, wash over us like a Category 5 hurricane. This is a life crisis so big there is no defense against it, no way of turning it aside, and no way to prevent all-out destruction.

How do we maintain our peace of soul through such a crisis? Doesn't Scripture tell us in countless passages in both Old and New Testaments: do not be afraid? And yet we continue to fear. This is not a character flaw; it's a deeply ingrained survival instinct. In addition, some people have the burden of past traumas or neurological illnesses that make it difficult to overcome fear. It's nothing to be ashamed of. Even Paul says, "I have the desire to do what is good, but I cannot carry it out." When Paul says he cannot do it, he means by his own strength alone.

Peace of soul in the midst of a crisis is a supernatural grace given by God. This is why Paul says the peace of God transcends all understanding. Grace transcends nature, adds God's strength to it, makes the impossible, possible.

How do we obtain this grace? By asking for it in prayer. Since grace is a gift of love that flows from the relationship we have with God, it is best to get to know God before the storm clouds gather. Like stocking our pantry and buying batteries when the weather is good, a regular habit of prayer strengthens us a little bit every day in preparation for hard times to come. But anytime is a good time to begin a relationship with God, even in the middle of a crisis.

My grandmother was certainly prepared for this crisis. She had a deep faith and a rich daily prayer life. Even though the experience of the storm was frightening, she trusted God completely. There is no doubt in my mind that the angels did indeed surround the house that night—with trees.

There is another lesson in peace of soul that can be gleaned from this story. Because my grandfather could not hear the terrible sounds of destruction, he was not disturbed by it. As it turns out, he didn't need to hear it; God was taking care of everything.

In this age of the internet, we can see and hear all sorts of literal and metaphorical storms going on all over the world. Every kind of catastrophe, illness, crime, war, and injustice can be streamed live before our eyes. Even the little storms of cheating spouses, bratty children, fighting neighbors, bridezillas, road rage, and bullying are posted for us to see.

The only person whose mission it is to bear all the sorrows of the world on his shoulders is Jesus Christ, our Lord. Not you, not I. We are not designed to see, hear, and know every horror in every nation, town, and home all over the world. These are not our storms to weather. This kind of knowledge is for God alone to bear, and we will feel our spirits darkening if we immerse ourselves in it.

But shouldn't we know what's going on in the world so that we can help those in need? Shouldn't we be alerted to troubles coming down the road so that we may avoid them or at least prepare for them? Of course. But there is a difference between knowing enough and knowing too much, discerning when we can help and when we can't, recognizing what concerns us and what's none of our business. Once again, grace is necessary. In our prayers for peace of soul, we should ask for the grace of wisdom to discern what knowledge to seek out for our good and what knowledge we should avoid.

Any time you face a crisis, consider praying Psalm 91, which is one of my favorite treasures of grace. As you read it, think about my grandmother's house, surrounded and sheltered by mighty trees during the storm. Better yet, fill your pantry now while the sun is shining. Consider adding Psalm 91 to your daily prayers. You will come to know it by heart, and it will easily spring to your lips when the next storm comes.

Storing Up Treasures in Heaven

Looking Within:
There are many blessings God wants to bestow on me if I will just ask. The help of the angels is one of those blessings. Every day, I will ask God to send his angels to help, protect and guide me, especially in times of crisis.

61

Prayer:

My Jesus, I ask for the grace of wisdom to discern what knowledge to seek out for my good and what knowledge I should avoid. Curb my curiosity about those things which are of no use to me and will only darken my spirit. Keep my soul at peace.

Tornado!
Finding Peace Before Future Catastrophes Strike
by Kira Marie McCullough

May 22, 2024. The sky appeared like a white-washed canvas. It was as if an artist had decided to rub the clouds from the picture; everything in the heavens had been obscured by a gray pall of fog dripping humidity and hiding the sun.

Despite the forecast of storms, I drove my car to the nearby retreat center where I like to worship on Wednesdays. I was greeted by an empty parking lot and a sign on the chapel door: *Church services are canceled through the end of May.*

Having nothing else to do, I decided to take a walk on the grounds. All was eerily still as I hiked the winding paths in the deepening shadows of overhanging trees. Heaviness and oppression filled the air like invisible specters of the underworld. Not a sliver of light patterned the path nor danced between the branches of cedars. Even the usually bright and cheerful wildflowers had closed their faces against the sky.

Thirty minutes later, thoroughly hot and sweaty, I got into my car and drove home. By the time I reached my apartment complex, it was 5:30 p.m. Curious about the weather, I pulled up a live video forecast online, only to be greeted by a rectangle of angry red blobs marching across the weather map, indicating severe thunderstorms headed towards my town; there were predictions of straight-line winds at 70 mph and large hail.

I had hoped to settle in for an evening of writing, but at that moment, the whining crescendo of the city's storm sirens erupted. At the same time, emergency weather alerts beeped from my cell phone. I knew these were warnings—a tornado had been spotted.

Quickly, I grabbed my painting of the Divine Mercy image of Jesus from the wall and set it in the bedroom windowsill. With trembling voice I said to the stormy sky beyond, "You have to go through Jesus to get to me!"

Closing all of the interior doors, I called my cat, Max (who followed compliantly, since I carried a bowl of kibble in one hand). I snatched my purse, computer, phone, and a few other things, and hurried to the bathroom where I crawled into the bathtub. I held a pillow against my chest, and positioned a large metal bowl on my head. My cat disappeared inside the lowest cabinet.

From the computer I heard the forecaster say: "A tornado has been spotted on Old Waco Road…"

My eyes widened with fear. I lived within a mile of Old Waco Road.

The lights flickered. *Off, on, off, on.*

The internet fizzled.

Abruptly, all power failed.

I was plunged into darkness.

An unnatural silence shrouded the space, as if the world held its breath. Then, as if letting go in an enormous exhale, the first wave of wind crashed against the house.

The earth shook with each booming thunderclap, and my skin crawled with the electric sizzling of lightning striking nearby trees. From beneath the door, a burst of light illuminated the hallway, causing me to speculate that a nearby transformer had been hit. The pouring rain turned to golf-ball sized hail beating the roof, like a herd of cattle stampeding across the prairie.

The entire episode lasted a mere fifteen minutes, but those minutes felt like an eternity. I prayed for my friends, for my neighbors, and my town. My heart throbbing, I squeaked out each prayer until my mouth grew dry and my brave prayers dissipated in the roaring storm, becoming dry whispers of "God save us!"

The pelting hailstones stopped. The roaring noise ceased. I heard only the steady falling of rain, as the thunder disappeared with the storm's march west.

I opened the bathroom door and went through my apartment. Satisfied that there had been no damage, I joined my neighbors outdoors. We checked our cars and explored the area littered with leafy tree branches and cluttered with leaves and twigs. Fences and trees all around us had been felled.

I was gladdened when I saw that my two enormous Live Oak trees, *Okie* and *Dokie*, still stood in splendor, like sentinels beside each of my windows, untouched by the gale. Picking my way carefully through tree limbs and water, I walked around the corner of the apartment complex to the other side. There, a ghastly sight met me. I stared incredulously at the tallest twin trees nearby. Each had been split in half from top to bottom, their burned inner bark a testament to lightning's fury. Their bowed crowns bent to the ground, the green jeweled leaves spreading silently, cast in a circle of twisted, tangled boughs. Had they fallen six inches closer to my apartment, they might have shattered my office window; had the wind launched them like a missile, they might have skewered the wall of my apartment.

Even the most astute planning could not have prevented the loss of those trees, and the many others uprooted that day. Even the most ardent of preppers could not have prevented the damage to hundreds of businesses and homes on that fateful afternoon when two tornadoes tore through my Texas town. Thankfully, not a single soul lost their life.

They say, "Don't be scared—be prepared." I had been both— ready with my homemade helmet (a metal bowl), tennis shoes, and a pillow. Yet, I had also been terrified. Shaking in the bathtub, I did not feel like a champion. Instead, I felt like a failure for being so scared. I could barely breath. I could scarcely speak; yet I did not quit crying out to God to save us.

Fear is a powerful emotion, and a natural feeling in dangerous situations. Even our Lord, Jesus, experienced excruciating fear in his human nature.

> *Then Jesus came with them to a place called Gethsemane, and he said to his disciples, "Sit here while I go over there and pray." He took along Peter and the two sons of Zebedee, and began to feel sorrow and distress. Then he said to them, "My soul is sorrowful even to death. Remain here and keep watch with me."*
>
> ~Matthew 26:36–38

The Garden of Gethsemane reveals the suffering of Christ, which was so severe that he sweated blood. This condition is labeled Hematidrosis, a rare disorder caused by the rupture of small vessels, triggered by extreme distress.

> *He was in such agony and he prayed so fervently that his sweat became like drops of blood falling on the ground.*
>
> ~Luke 22:44

> *After withdrawing about a stone's throw from them and kneeling, he prayed, saying, "Father, if you are willing, take this cup away from me; still, not my will but yours be done."*
>
> ~Luke 22:41, 42

Fully God and fully man, Jesus suffered *perfectly*. He experienced mortal fear in the garden, yet his divine Love—for the Father and for us—cast this fear into the molten furnace of the Divine Will, and the burnished gold of his fiat resounds throughout eternity.

Scripture declares that "Perfect love casts out all fear." (1 John 4:18). Jesus prayed in agony in the garden, then rose to his feet, facing the Cross with complete love and humility. As human beings, this is impossible for us—unless we are infused by God's grace.

Riding out the tornadoes in my bathtub, I panicked, thinking that the roof would cave in on top of me, or the apartment would blow away. I could hardly hear my own tiny voice squeaking, "Save us!" My anxiety reached a height greater than the depth of my trust in God. I had prepared physically, but I had not been prepared for the onslaught of a dreadful panic more potent than any fear I had ever experienced.

Since then, I have had to ask myself this hard question: How will I face potential, unexpected tragedies with less fear and more confidence in God? After all, Texas is no stranger to natural disasters; its landscape has been ravaged by wildfires and hurricanes, floods, and ice storms. Such weather-related events seem to be increasing everywhere.

The only answer is to trust God, more

Had I recognized the permissive will of God at work, had I leaned more upon his divine wisdom, had I expected his great protection (whether through life or death), I would have been less anxious on the day the tornadoes rattled my home and my sensibilities.

I have learned that the secret to sailing through stormy seas is to make ready the ship of my soul. Before calamities come, I must store within my heart the treasures of grace—a peacefulness based on a childlike, loving trust in the goodness of God.

How do we do this, you ask? Is it even possible to be prepared for the unexpected? Is it really reasonable to think that we could face catastrophes with little or no fear?

Remember that grace is a supernatural gift from God, lifting us out of our natural tendencies and fears—even if momentarily. The stories of the early Christian martyrs facing lions in the Roman arena with tranquility and unperturbed faith are a testament to God's grace. Then there was the Old Testament figure, Daniel, who was thrown into the lion's den—he offered himself to God in prayer, and the Lord caused the vicious animals to become tame as house cats.

The stories in the bible and our own experience tell us that trials and tribulations are guaranteed in this life. Therefore, my goal is to trust God more when future winds and waves assail. I cannot guarantee that the next time a storm appears on the horizon I will walk on water—like Peter, I may sink beneath my doubts, crying, "God, save us!"

However, a lofty goal is not necessarily an unattainable goal—especially with God's treasure of grace pouring undeserved into our souls, hearts, and minds. Remember, Peter—who sank beneath the waves and later denied Christ three times—became the Rock upon which Jesus built his Church. Our past failures do not prevent God from giving us future victories, if we will only *trust him more.*

God is in control—not the weather.

God is in control—not my fear.

Whether through life or death, God's love is like a trustworthy ship carrying us through the storms of tragedy, difficulty, and fear.

> *For if we live, we live for the Lord, and if we die, we die for the Lord; so then, whether we live or die, we are the Lord's.*
>
> ~Romans 14:8

Storing Up Treasures in Heaven

Prepare your soul for future events by meditating on verses that strengthen your trust in God. Below are two Bible passages that have been supremely helpful to me. First, Psalm 139 shows God's great love, which is unique and individual. Second, there is the passage about Jesus asleep in the boat, which reassures us of his divine power even in the face of our doubts and weakness.

When we embrace both the amazing love and awe-inspiring power of God, we receive greater grace in our lives, leading us to believe more in his Divine Providence. Our souls are better equipped for anything that might happen.

Though fear is natural (and we should not be ashamed when we feel frightened), it need not *control* us—for Jesus, Himself, is steering our little boat through the turbulent seas of life's tribulations, bringing us safely to the harbor of peace and goodness.

Lord, you have probed me, you know me:
  you know when I sit and stand;
  you understand my thoughts from afar.
You sift through my travels and my rest;
  with all my ways you are familiar.
Even before a word is on my tongue,
  Lord, you know it all.
Behind and before you encircle me
  and rest your hand upon me.
Such knowledge is too wonderful for me,
  far too lofty for me to reach.
Where can I go from your spirit?
  From your presence, where can I flee?
If I ascend to the heavens, you are there;
  if I lie down in Sheol, there you are.
If I take the wings of dawn
  and dwell beyond the sea,
Even there your hand guides me,
  your right hand holds me fast.
If I say, "Surely darkness shall hide me,
  and night shall be my light"—
Darkness is not dark for you,
  and night shines as the day.
  Darkness and light are but one.

You formed my inmost being;
  you knit me in my mother's womb.

69

I praise you, because I am wonderfully made;
wonderful are your works!
My very self you know.
My bones are not hidden from you,
When I was being made in secret,
fashioned in the depths of the earth.
Your eyes saw me unformed;
in your book all are written down;
my days were shaped, before one came to be.

How precious to me are your designs, O God;
how vast the sum of them!
Were I to count them, they would outnumber the sands;
when I complete them, still you are with me.
When you would destroy the wicked, O God,
the bloodthirsty depart from me!
Your foes who conspire a plot against you
are exalted in vain.

Do I not hate, Lord, those who hate you?
Those who rise against you, do I not loathe?
With fierce hatred I hate them,
enemies I count as my own.
Probe me, God, know my heart;
try me, know my thoughts.
See if there is a wicked path in me;
lead me along an ancient path.

~Psalm 139

He got into a boat and his disciples followed him. Sud-
denly a violent storm came up on the sea, so that the boat
was being swamped by waves; but he was asleep. They
came and woke him, saying, "Lord, save us! We are per-
ishing!" He said to them, "Why are you terrified, O you of

little faith?" Then he got up, rebuked the winds and the sea, and there was great calm. The men were amazed and said, "What sort of man is this, whom even the winds and the sea obey?"

~Matthew 8: 23–27

IF THE TIME COMES
Peace in Times of Persecution
by Keb Burns

I hope and pray that you never need to use this meditation. But if the time comes, I also hope and pray that you will remember this.

After three years traveling with his Apostles, the time had come for Jesus to leave them. He knew that what was coming was going to be horrifying for them to witness, and their faith would be put to the ultimate test. He also knew what they would face after he left them on their own, to continue his work without him. All would face persecution. All but one would be martyred. How do you prepare someone for something like that? What could he say to give them strength to bear up under the sorrow and suffering they would face?

In the 16th chapter of John, we see that he shares one last Passover supper with them. He knows that by the following evening, he will be sealed in a tomb after a long and terrible execution. The Apostles do not know this. We see how gently Jesus tried to prepare them for what was coming. After a long discourse, he said:

> *"I have told you this so that you might have peace in me."*
> ~John 16:33

Wait, what did he say there? He said he wants them to face their troubles at peace, he wants them to face persecution at peace, he wants them to face martyrdom at peace. Remember this. If the time should come when you must face these things, he wants you to face them at peace, too.

Hopefully, this kind of trouble will never come. But we all face small forms of persecution from time to time. The relative who makes fun of our faith at the Thanksgiving family gathering, the atheist teacher who, in class, makes fun of the students who believe in God, the co-workers who bash the denomination we belong to, the friends who ridicule us for following the Ten Commandments, the spouse who pressures the family to stay home on Sunday instead of going to church, the unbelieving grandparents who influence our children behind our backs, the boss who insults our faith and forbids us to respond.

When these things happen, Jesus wants us to be at peace and handle it in a peaceful manner. If persecution of a more serious, organized nature comes, we will want to be at peace with our fellow Christians, as well. That means we must learn how to be at peace with them now. We can't be guilty of persecuting others for their faith if we want others to be tolerant of ours. It is one thing to draw comparisons between beliefs in a respectful discussion; it is quite another thing to insult, ridicule, or degrade the beliefs that others hold dear. If real persecution should come, we will all need to support each other in charity.

Jesus began his final instructions with the words, "I am the Vine; you are the branches...apart from me you can do nothing." We can't face persecution alone. We must cling as tightly to Christ as a branch to a vine. Daily prayer keeps the branch firmly attached to the vine. If we let go of prayer, persecution will carry us away like a withered leaf in the wind.

Storing Up Treasures in Heaven

Looking Within:
Jesus' final prayer for his disciples is found in John 17:6-26. Today, I see myself sitting at the table with Jesus and the Apostles in

the Upper Room. As I read this passage, I know that He is praying to the Eternal Father for the Apostles…and for me! While he is praying, he knows the trouble that is coming for the Apostles. He also knows about all the troubles that are coming in my future, too. These words are for me. When trouble comes, Jesus wants me to stay closely united to him and to the Father and to remember that my ultimate destiny is to be with him in Heaven. Jesus wants me to find my peace in this destiny.

Prayer:

My Jesus, I ask for the grace to be at peace with those whose beliefs are different from mine while also having the courage to never betray my own. Fill my soul with peace as you strengthen my faith.

PART 5

When You are Anxious and Fearful
Creating Peace Now and Later

PLUNGING UNDER THE WATER
Taking Back Peace when Fears Assail
by Kira Marie McCullough

I shivered in the cold water, bobbing up and down on my tippy toes. My chin shook, and my teeth clattered. My arms flailed, and I gasped. To the casual observer, it might have appeared as if I were drowning, but in actuality, I was preparing for the biggest plunge of my life.

This marked the first day of swimming lessons, and as a spunky four-year-old, I was determined to dive under before the teacher forced me to. As the pool water stung my eyes and sloshed into my mouth, I recalled the conversation with my mother earlier that morning.

"Today, you are going to learn how to swim," she had said with a smile, while brushing my long brunette hair into a pony tail.

I had already donned my bathing suit and had a large towel wrapped about me. "What does that mean?" I asked, wincing as she bound my thick curls with a tight rubber band.

"That means that you will be able to plug your nose, hold your breath, and put your head under the water and move around the pool like a fish."

Mortified, I cried, "Ouch!"—not only because of the painful stretching of the rubber band that pulled the tiny hairs at the back of my neck, but at the thought of having to *hold my breath* underwater. My imagination went wild. If I was going to become an animal, I preferred the idea of becoming a land mammal. I loved the thought of being a frisky horse, galloping through the fields of dandelions near our home—not a slimy fish slithering in the depths of a green pool, devoid of oxygen.

"You don't have a choice," my mother said. "You need to learn how to swim."

Because it was inevitable, I began preparing myself mentally for the plunge. I pictured each step, from pinching my nose to closing my eyes to making the final dive. This imagery rolled over and over in my mind as my mother drove us across town.

It was a hot morning in our small Kansas town when we traipsed into the swim teacher's backyard, a motley crew of kids in bathing suits, carrying towels. While our parents waited on the patio, we climbed the ladder to a platform overlooking the water. Our teacher was a burly football coach from the local high school, who taught children in his above ground pool during the summer. The coach jumped in, and then helped each of us settle on our feet.

I remember how the water swilled around us, making the corrugated blue sides seem to bend and sway. I was immersed in shimmering azure, with blue plastic pale and watery beneath my feet, becoming a sun-speckled indigo as the plastic stretched up the sides of the pool. I considered my options. I could wait to be dipped underwater, or take the plunge on my own. The fear of the coach's meaty hands pressing down on my head frightened me more than the idea of doing it myself.

When the coach looked away, I squeezed my nose between my fingers, with eyes wide open, and lurched downward, bending my knees until my head had been completely submerged. The roaring in my ears surprised me. The wavy images of legs amazed me. Suddenly, I jumped up, pushing off the bottom with my feet, opening my mouth to gasp for air and flinging my wet hair, shaking the droplets on the startled faces around me.

My teacher's eyebrows shot up with genuine shock. Pleased that I had not required rescuing, (having survived my own dunking), he smiled broadly and exclaimed, "Good job!"

Proud and shivering, I grinned, showing my missing two front teeth. I had overcome my fear. Rather than waiting for the coach to push my head under the water, I had done it myself. On my own terms. And it seemed like he was mighty impressed.

That was the first and last scary day of swimming lessons. From then on, I eagerly followed instructions, learning how to hold onto the platform and kick my legs furiously, float on my back delightedly, and doggy paddle back and forth across the water vigorously.

Fear can either paralyze us, or spur us to action in good ways

If I had been given the choice by my mother, I would have skipped swimming lessons entirely, resulting in a lifetime of regret. I would have never enjoyed swimming in the cold waters of Lake Erie as a young girl, or paddling my raft on a pond in Arkansas as a pre-teen; I would have denied myself a full-body bath in the warm waves of the Gulf of Mexico, or the hike with my daughter that took us fearlessly, hip-deep, into the rushing streams of California's redwood forests.

Although fear is a natural emotion, sometimes supernatural grace is needed to overcome it. We face fearful situations throughout our lifetimes, sometimes daily. I have discovered that there are two kinds of fear:

- *Rational fear.* This fear is grounded in reality. It is a life-saving gift from God to spare us from danger, and by his grace we overcome each obstacle through courage, persistence, and fortitude. Rational fears are usually resolved by taking appropriate action.
- *Imaginary fear.* This fear has no visible cause. It is a vague anxiety of doom, sent by the enemy of our souls to keep us from making life-giving choices. Imaginary fears may not always go away, yet the battle can be won daily by submitting to God and resisting fear's temptations.

When my children were little, they were occasionally frightened of their darkened bedrooms where imaginary monsters lurked. I would reassure them with one of my favorite scripture passages:

> *For God did not give us a spirit of cowardice but rather of power and love and self-control.*
>
> ~2 Timothy 1:7

Confronting my fear of the water required great courage for a little girl. As a child, I needed to develop a new skill-set as a swimmer in order to have a future filled with watery experiences that did not scare me. I needed to make peace with the water, in order to master my fears. My anxiety was real, and through appropriate action (putting my head under the water; following my teacher's directions; daily practicing the techniques), the fears disappeared, replaced by confidence.

As a grown woman, I have developed a new set of skills that helps me navigate both the rational and irrational fears of my life. I have learned that mastery is possible and peace attainable—whether facing a tornado barreling across town towards my house (a real fear) or a vague nervousness I feel when sitting on the front row at church, worried of what people are thinking about me (an imaginary fear).

This new skill set begins with the recognition of who God is—and who I am in relationship to him. He is the Creator—I am the creature in need of his love. He is the Redeemer—I am the sinner in need of his salvation. He is the Sanctifier—I am the beloved child in need of holiness. Knowing that God is all-powerful and all-loving, I can rest in his care, trusting that he will guide me through every fear, whether real or imagined.

This means my life is going to be a series of lessons, allowed by God, designed to teach me to receive and give love, and make me holy in the process. Like the burly coach who taught us to swim, God puts me into the pool of life's experiences in order to train me to turn to him with trust.

Certain problems must be encountered head on—there is no way around them. No detour. We must plug our noses, close our eyes, and plunge down to the depths of our difficulties, trusting God that we will rise above them with the glorious victory of overcoming our challenges.

The reward for facing our fears is peace.

Storing Up Treasures in Heaven

If you are confronting frightening circumstances—standing chin-deep in a gigantic pool of splashing water, afraid to swim—*pray*. Begin by asking God for *courage*. Admit to him that you are floundering. Ask him for the *power, love,* and *sound mind* that he promises in II Timothy 1:7. Seek his wisdom to take right action.

After prayer, it is time to make the best decision you can possibly make. Whether choosing to take college classes or learning to drive a car, every bold choice we make will strengthen our confidence in both God and our own abilities. If your decisions bring peace, you know that you were facing a real fear.

However, if the anxiety continues, you may be dealing with an irrational fear. Go to God in prayer and submit yourself to his tender mercies; ask him for the power to resist the lies of the enemy; seek his strength to stand firmly against the onslaught of fear, which tempts us to make rash choices in panic, rather than faith. Turn to scripture, friends, and the church for wisdom and guidance, so you may take back the peace that is your inheritance, the gift God desires to give all of his children.

> *Peace I leave with you; my peace I give to you. Not as the world gives do I give it to you. Do not let your hearts be troubled or afraid.*
>
> ~John 14:27

Pumpkin Seeds
At Peace with Paradise Lost

by Keb Burns

I had fallen into an exhausted sleep on the couch after several hours of work on a greeting card design for a client. The project wasn't difficult, and I had enjoyed doing it, but for some reason it had drained me of all my energy. Maybe I was coming down with something.

This was a deeply happy time in my life. I was in the early years of building what I hoped would be a career in commercial art. Life was exactly what I dreamed it would be: setting up my attic studio, selling my work, listening to classical music as I painted late into the night, walking my dog on a crisp fall day, playing the piano, dressing up and going out with friends, sharing all of our exciting plans for the future. We were all going to travel the world and then conquer it. At twenty-one, life was just beginning and for me it was paradise.

Around midnight, I woke up nauseous and then began vomiting. Normally I would say this was nothing to worry about since I was at the peak of health, strength, and youth, but this did not feel like an ordinary cold or flu. I felt peculiar...and terrible. In the back of my mind alarm bells were ringing.

"There's something wrong," I told my mom, "...very wrong. I think you'd better call an ambulance."

In the emergency room, the doctors hooked me up to an EKG machine; apparently my heart was misbehaving. My skin and eyes were jaundiced. My kidneys were struggling. I couldn't think straight, and I was in pain. It felt like all my bones were broken and

81

all my muscles were bruised. Whatever this was, it was attacking my whole body. "You have a very sick little girl here," one of the doctors told my parents.

In spite of all this, I was at peace because I trusted that the doctors would figure it out and fix it. This was a new decade, the 1970s. We conquered the moon; space age medicine could fix everything, right? For the rest of the night and late into the next day, a team of doctors ran test after test. Finally, one of them came in to talk to me.

"We thought you had leukemia, but tests ruled that out. Our consensus is that you probably have some kind of infection. Since your symptoms have subsided over the last few hours, we're going to send you home with antibiotics."

He turned to go but then hesitated and turned back. "I'm going to be honest with you. Personally, I don't think this is an infection. Your white cell count is too high for that. In fact, it's the highest I've ever seen in any patient. I think you have something else. I just don't know what it is or what more to test you for."

How right he was! Though I didn't know it then, my brief time in paradise had just ended. After I got home, I never quite bounced back. The jaundice would come and go, as would rashes, shortness of breath, pinching pain in my liver and spleen, episodes of nausea and vomiting, splitting headaches, brain fog, and memory loss. The profound fatigue and muscle pain never went away. Neither did the sleep disturbances. I would either sleep for hours without refreshment or not be able to sleep at all. I had to budget my energy each day the way most people have to budget their money. Do I wash dishes or do laundry? I didn't have the energy for both. There were many days I didn't have the energy to get out of bed or even eat. At other times, symptoms subsided, and I felt well enough to return to my work. Unfortunately, I never knew which me was going to show up when I woke in the morning.

About a year later I again found myself in the emergency room with the same constellation of symptoms as before. Again, the tests were inconclusive, the symptoms subsided on their own, and they sent me home without a diagnosis. They also gave me referrals to specialists in cardiology, urology, gastroenterology, internal medicine, and even psychiatry—just in case it was all in my head (how can jaundice be all in your head?). I naively thought all of these doctors were collaborating to pinpoint one mysterious ailment. I was wrong.

I vividly remember the day I kept the appointment with the urologist and recited all my symptoms to him. He didn't seem to be listening. He also had the hospital record, but he barely glanced at it. He told me I probably had an infection and prescribed an antibiotic. "But what about my heart and my jaundice and swollen joints and all the other symptoms?" I asked. He looked at me as if I were the dumbest person in the world and said "Your heart? How should I know? I'm not a cardiologist. What does your heart have to do with your kidneys?"

The medical theory of the day said that hearts had nothing to do with kidneys and livers had nothing to do with lungs and skin had nothing to do with the gut. That's why they couldn't diagnose me. At that moment I realized that no one was going to fix this because no one knew how. Now I was scared. I went home in tears.

I continued to seek answers from various doctors as my symptoms flared and remitted and my ability to function declined, but all of them said the same thing: "You definitely have something, but I'm not sure what it is." I had an illness with no name, no explanation, and no end in sight. This continued for years, and my condition deteriorated. I fell into a deep depression as I began to fear that I would never know the answer and never be well again. For all I knew, it might even be fatal.

Finally, I turned it all over to God and gave him my life completely. I told him that if he wanted to take everything away from me, even my life, I accepted. All I asked was that he would show me how to make this truncated life useful to him in some

83

way. And that is when everything changed. A deep peace came over me and I was no longer afraid.

One day shortly after this prayer, I was on the patio scooping seeds out of a pumpkin to make a jack-o-lantern. It suddenly struck me that each one of these seeds was a potential new plant…and there were hundreds of seeds in this one pumpkin. I glanced up at the plum, pomegranate, and pear trees in our yard and recalled the hundreds of fruits they produced every year. All of these fruits contained thousands of seeds that could sprout new trees. I tried to calculate how many trees could come from these fruits year after year. Fractals of unending generations of trees extended as far out in time as my boggled mind could imagine. God's generosity overwhelmed me. Why so much abundance, I wondered?

But of course! God is an infinite Being. Infinite means "without limits." The universe is exploding with unending abundance because that's the natural result of having no limits. An infinite God can't stop being infinite. In fact, an infinite God can't stop being anything. It's his nature to be an ever-flowing fountain of life.

This abundance is everywhere: in billions of stars and galaxies, in the animal kingdom, in the ocean, and even…I suddenly realized…in my life, too. I had been thinking that God had taken everything away from me, that his abundance toward me had stopped. But that was impossible. Did I seriously think that his infinite nature would suddenly come to a screeching halt just because it reached my door? God must still be pouring infinite abundance into my life right now, just as he does everywhere else. He can't help himself; it's who he is.

It's true that the plan I mapped out for my life was gone. But that was just one plan. I had been acting like the entire universe had gone dark because a single star had winked out while there were still billions of galaxies all around me. All I had to do was open my eyes and see the abundance that was still being poured into my life. Once I knew what to look for, it was easy to see.

I was given an abundance of time.

Long months sick in bed gave me the time to read all the wonderful books that caught my eye in the library. Through the interlibrary loan program, I ordered rare and special books from libraries and universities all over the country. I gained an amazing education in theology, science, art, horticulture, music, history, and a zillion arcane subjects that are not in any college curriculum.

I was given an abundance of solitude.

My healthy friends moved on with their lives. No one could understand or relate to what was happening to me. In their place, God stepped in and kept me company. Through long hours of prayer and contemplation, I came to know God in ways I never would have if I had pursued my busy career plans. I also found a way to make my life useful by praying for family, friends, neighbors, and strangers. Since they were too busy to pray for themselves, I stepped in and prayed for all their many needs. I would not trade those hours now for anything in the world

I was given an abundance of something I dearly needed.

Illness offered me plenty of opportunities to learn patience, compassion, and humility. When I finally let go of my plan to acquire an abundance of things, money, and admiration, God gave me something more valuable, a fertile field to plant a thousand pumpkin seeds of virtue.

So, did I ever find out what my mysterious condition is? In recent years medicine has changed its philosophy of disease. The body isn't just a collection of parts thrown together in a bag; it's a complex, interdependent system. Because of this new understanding, I finally got a diagnosis. I have an autoimmune condition that is currently incurable, occasionally fatal, but manageable with strict lifestyle modifications. I now stay mostly in remission and live a mostly normal life.

Storing Up Treasures in Heaven

Looking Within:

Even though my life has not gone according to what I planned, I know that if I give my life to God, he will fill the void with an abundance of other kinds of blessings. He can't help himself; it's who he is.

Prayer:

My Jesus, open my eyes to the abundance you are pouring into my life. Show me all the things I can do with that abundance. Just like me, many people have had to give up cherished dreams because of unhappy circumstances: illness, accident, divorce, death of a loved one, loss of income, or disability. Give me an abundance of compassion for those who are grieving these painful losses and show me how to overflow the abundance you are giving me into their lives.

PART 6

When Someone You Love Dies
Finding Peace in the Midst of Grief

WHEN YOU LOSE YOUR BEST FRIEND
Finding Peace after Loss
by Kira Marie McCullough

I am thankful for the technological advances that have produced a portable cell phone—a virtual high-tech wizard that serves as an alarm clock, encyclopedia, mailbox, and camera. The camera, to me, is the best part. And if you are as old as I am, you'll understand this metaphor: Today's cell phones are a mini-scrapbook album, a sort of a digitized version of the bulky books of parchment paper that we used to fill with snapshots and memorabilia.

Scrapbooks were the rage when I was growing up. I still have a few with high school photos of old boyfriends, birthday party invitations, and blue ribbons won from piano contests, all carefully attached with scotch tape or a thin line of Elmer's glue. I can take the dusty photo albums from the closet whenever I choose, and sometimes, I choose to let them sit dusty and unopened for years.

My phone, however, seems to have a mind of its own. Daily, the screen pops up with images I snapped in the past, with taglines like, "On this day three years ago." Usually, I ignore these invitations. But on May 26, 2024, I unexpectedly found myself staring at the photographs of my 87-year-old father, Charles. Though he had died five years earlier, there he was, sitting on a camp chair beneath a tarp at my niece's *Sweet Sixteen* birthday party at my sister's farm near San Antonio.

The pictures produced bittersweet memories. With fondness, I recalled his conversation with my mother, who sat nearby.

I could see his red-rimmed eyes, his crooked smile, his calm and alert presence as he watched the grandchildren play in the pool. I remembered the tentative way he removed and readjusted his cap, over and over, bringing cool air to his skin. I recalled my last moment with him, when I leaned over and kissed the soft, baby-like flesh of his balding head, noticing the thinning hair.

"I love you, Dad," I whispered.

He winked, nodded, and smiled with affection, replying in a voice husky with age, "I love you, too."

That would be our last encounter before his death, and later, would become the inspiration for the short story, "Her Best Kiss" (*King of the Lake and Other Stories*, Wordcrafts Press). Two weeks after snapping those pictures, my father entered hospice care in his home, and died peacefully in his bed on June 8, 2019.

The loss seemed more than I could bear. For the eight years prior, I had called my dad my "best friend." This is remarkable considering the fact that for most of my adult life, my father and I rarely enjoyed being around each other. When my family lived a thousand miles away, conversations with my dad were mostly through the old rotary phone. We disagreed on politics. We argued about religion. We sparred over ethics. We made one another cry. We hung up on each other.

Yet, over the years, unbeknownst to either of us, God was working in the hidden places of our hearts, removing the little stones of contention, smoothing the rocky ground of unforgiveness. A thousand miles away, over the course of twenty-five years, my father was slowly embracing God's love and forgiveness, and so was I.

This silent coup by God won a victory over our souls, and suddenly, after more than two decades of quarreling, the miraculous happened:

We quit hanging up the phone.

We began to talk freely, without squabbling.

We listened to one-another, without judgment.

My father offered sage advice that guided me in making important decisions.

The truth of this Proverb bloomed in my life, and I rejoiced:

Oil and perfume rejoice the heart; So doth the sweetness of a man's friend that cometh of hearty counsel.
~Proverbs 27:9

I quit seeing my dad as a project to fix, and my father stopped treating me as a high school debater. With neither of us needing to protect fragile egos anymore, he encouraged me by saying, "You are so talented," or "I am very proud of you," or "Never give up." When I was jobless, he asked his Sunday School class to pray for me, and when I had no money in my pocket, he invited me to visit his little stone house in Helotes where the food was free and the guest bedroom a safe haven from the storms of life.

In the mornings there would be percolating coffee, toasted bread with sweet margarine and grape jelly, and the two of us at the kitchen table with my daddy's notebook beside him. In his journal, he notated the activities of the day. He would tell me stories of the Great Depression when milk was delivered by the milk man in ice-cold bottles, and Karo syrup was the sweetener of choice.

I never tired of hearing about the time he had hitchhiked from his tiny town in Indiana to the nearby college, without a penny to his name. The admissions counselor had asked, "How will you pay?" My father answered, "God will provide." And that step of faith began his four years of university work.

In 2019, though I knew that he was dying, I was not ready for the impact of actually losing my best friend. After the news of his death, I tumbled into a year of grieving, marked by fatigue and the onset of vertigo. I lost both my physical and spiritual balance. My steadying pillar of a father had been removed, and my life crumbled. Rather than sink into complete despair, I reached out for help. Prayer, church, and friends helped me pick up the pieces. In my mourning, I leaned upon my Heavenly Father.

> *Though my flesh and my heart fail,*
>   *God is the rock of my heart, my portion forever.*
>   ~Psalm 73:26

For most of us, the journey of loss will be taken over and over, again. My father was not the first. I have grieved over grandparents, aunts and uncles, friends, and even our firstborn child.

Yet, God did not leave me in despair.

> *When I say, "My foot is slipping,"*
>   *your mercy, Lord, holds me up.*
> *When cares increase within me,*
>   *your comfort gives me joy.*
>   ~Psalm 94:18, 19

God does not promise us a life free of pain and suffering. What he promises is that he will be with us, strengthening our hearts, restoring our souls, and healing our brokenness.

> *Blessed are they who mourn, for they will be comforted.*
>   ~Matthew 5:4

The Bible teaches us that the death of the body means the separation of our soul from our physical being—but only for a brief time. God promises a glorious resurrection of all dead bodies, to be reunited with their souls, at the end of time. This means that one day, I will once again hold my father's strong hand in mine.

> *But now Christ has been raised from the dead, the*

firstfruits[a] of those who have fallen asleep. For since death came through a human being, the resurrection of the dead came also through a human being.

~1 Corinthians 15: 20, 21

Knowing that death is not the end is the key to finding peace in the midst of loss.

He will wipe every tear from their eyes, and there shall be no more death or mourning, wailing or pain, [for] the old order has passed away.

~Revelation 21:4

Walking into the future without our best friend—whether we have buried a beloved father, mother, sister, brother, or spouse—necessitates heroic courage. Ask God to help you be brave. Since my father's death, I have learned how to make decisions without his guidance; I have found friends who applaud my successes and cheer for me in my struggles; when I want to pick up the phone and call my dad, I stop and pray, realizing God still speaks to me, even in the absence of the one I love.

I owe my father a life well-lived. He would be proud of me for going on without him, growing in faith, hope, and charity, in pursuit of the goodness of God. He would want me to use my talents and love others.

Storing Up Treasures in Heaven

Today, spend time in prayer, thanking God for the relationship you had with the person you loved and lost; ask God to tenderly carry your best friend to Heaven; ask the Lord to help you carry the burden of your sorrow; and then, spend time in silence, listening for the new hopes and dreams stirring in your imagination. Believe that God has a future for you worth living.

For I know well the plans I have in mind for you—oracle of the Lord—plans for your welfare and not for woe, so as to give you a future of hope..

~Jeremiah 29:11

THE WASHING MACHINE
At Peace with Caregiving

by Keb Burns

My mother looked like the 1930s edition of the Campbell's Soup Kid with her round face, rosy cheeks and bowl haircut. Her name was Kathleen, but the family called her Kath. At age five she was a wild, barefoot tomboy in worn-out overalls, following her wilder older brother around, imitating his pranks. Even in the isolation of their parents' homestead in the Colorado foothills, she and Buddy could find the most ingenious trouble to get into. An old black-and-white photo taken at the time shows them looking like a couple of ragged, dusty characters from *The Grapes of Wrath*, peering at the camera with stern faces. Their two older sisters were only slightly daintier in their calico dresses, but all four of them stared into the camera with no-nonsense expressions that seemed to say, "Life is hard but we can handle it."

Kath knew her brother had put a dead lizard in the pocket of his overalls, but she had forgotten about it. Apparently, so had he. When she heard a woman scream that summer morning, Kath ran around the house to the back yard to see her mother standing at the galvanized washtub with a pair of wet overalls in one hand and some unrecognizable goo in the other. The overalls were pressed flat, having just gone through the wringer that was clamped to the edge of the tub. Kath remembered the lizard and grasped what had happened.

"That's it! That's it," her mother yelled. "Fred, Fred come out here and look at this!" Her dad was already on his way out the back door, having heard the scream. The screen door slapped behind him. Though he towered over his wife, he seemed to shrink during the next few minutes. The tiny woman exploded into a rambling, tearful, stream-of-consciousness tirade about work and laundry and long hours of endless cooking.

Kath was confused; she suspected that, somehow, this was no longer about a dead lizard. "Fred, I need an electric washing machine" her mother said, wiping tears from her eyes. "I've been looking at the Sears catalog. We can go into town and order it, and it can be here in four weeks." There was an edge of desperation in her voice.

Fred gasped. "Agnes, we can't afford it! You know we can't."

Kath didn't know what the Great Depression was. All she knew was that life had always been good, and then suddenly it wasn't. Her dad had worked long hours on the trucking business he had started, and he had done well at first. Then, one October day in 1929, something bad was on the front page of the newspaper, and now, instead of having his own business, he had to work for the electric company, climbing power poles at all hours, sometimes in the middle of a Denver snowstorm.

"I can't go on doing laundry by hand. It's killing my back, it takes up all my time, I can't get the other chores done, my hands are cracked and bleeding—I just can't do it anymore!"

Fred praised her for being strong. He said something about how hard he was working too and that together they would get through it somehow. That seemed to help a little and she began to calm down. Kath thought her dad should have quit talking right there. Unfortunately, he didn't. Though he was trying to be encouraging, he made the mistake of adding:

"My mother did laundry in a washtub for all eight of us kids all of her married life, and if she could do it, you can do it too."

Splash went the overalls back into the tub. "Well, I've done as much of it as I'm going to do in my married life!" She stormed into the house.

Kath heard a door slam somewhere inside. She was scared.

She had never heard her parents argue or even raise their voices to each other. Her mother didn't come out of her room for the rest of the night.

In the morning Dad was making breakfast. "Where's Mom?" Buddy asked. Dad sighed and remained silent for a moment. Finally, in a low voice he said, "She went to visit your Grandma and Grandpa."

Kath, in a trembling voice, asked, "When is she coming back?" Her dad just shrugged his shoulders.

Mom was gone for a month. During that time Dad divided up the chores among all four kids, partly to keep them busy while he was away at work and partly because he couldn't do them all himself. The two older girls were responsible for washing the dishes, picking up, making beds, cooking, and sweeping. Buddy was expected to take care of the market garden, dig potatoes, bring water from the well, and keep the birds away from the fruit trees. Kath had to feed and water the chickens and collect the eggs from the hen house. She hated those chores because the rooster chased her, and the hens pecked at her hands. Dad took the hardest jobs for himself. He did the twice-a-day milking, the wood-chopping, the floor-mopping, and, yes, the laundry.

One day, Kath was sitting on the back porch watching him pull heavy, wet overalls out of the washtub and scrub them on the rippled washboard. She was blowing fluff from a dandelion when she noticed him stand up straight, put his hands on the small of his back, stretch backwards and groan. Suddenly with a look of firm determination he strode off into the barn and slammed the barn door behind him. When Kath heard the clatter and clang of iron, she knew he was at his workbench.

At twilight he came into the house to get a lantern and to tell the girls to not fix him any dinner. He wasn't hungry, he told them. He went back into the barn and stayed late into the night. Kath put herself to bed that night, feeling lonely and neglected without her father's goodnight kiss.

The next day before going off to work, her dad strictly ordered all four kids to stay out of the barn. He used the same tone of voice he used the time he caught Kath trying to reach something on the hot stove. That was his, *I mean business!* voice. Every night after work, Dad inhaled his dinner and then disappeared into the barn.

Summer was winking at autumn when her mom came home. A neighbor picked her up at the train station and brought her to the house. She got out of the car, set her suitcase on the ground, thanked the neighbor, and waved as the car drove away. All four kids ran to her, hugged her, and talked all at once. Then they stood back as they noticed a tension in the air. Dad had come out on the front porch, and he and Mom were looking at each other in silence. After an awkward pause Dad said, "Come into the house and sit in the kitchen a minute. I have something to show you." Mom and all the kids went into the kitchen and sat at the table while Dad went out to the barn.

Soon, they all heard the squeaking wheels of dad's hand truck coming across the yard. Kath and Buddy jumped up to run to the door, but Mom sternly ordered them to sit back down.

After a few grunts and clanks from out in the yard there was a moment of silence. Then Dad's voice called, "OK! Come out and see." Mom led the troop out onto the back porch. There, in the grass, next to a sheepish husband sat a home-built, electrically-powered washing machine, cobbled together out of scavenged parts. Mother was speechless for a moment, then she flew off the porch and threw her arms around him.

"I'm so sorry, Agnes," Fred told her. "I had no idea how hard it was."

Many years later, Kath sat with her father in another kitchen, in another town, in another time. She was now grown up with a husband and kids of her own. As dementia and then cancer gradually robbed her mother of the ability to do chores around the house, her dad picked them up, one by one. His days and nights were consumed by housework and caregiving until finally, one evening, he had called Kath on the phone to tell her, "The cross is too heavy, I can't carry it anymore." He had to let his beloved Agnes go to be cared for in a professional setting, where she passed away.

Her mother had been buried that day and Kath was keeping her father company that evening. Sitting at the kitchen table with an album of old photos, he had nothing but happy memories. Pointing to a photo, he laughed and said "Look at you four. You look like a bunch of hooligans. That was taken in front of our house in Colorado," he said. He turned a page. "There's me and your mom. Look how young we were. Just a couple of kids. And there's that old washing machine I built for your mother…"

Suddenly he stopped, turned to his daughter and said, "I miss my cross."

"I know, Dad, I know," she answered, patting him on the shoulder. He gazed through the window, off into the distance, his mind evidently on a far-away memory. Then he turned to her and smiled.

"Don't worry, Kath, I'm at peace because I know I did all I could. And I was happy to take care of her. I would do it again. It was the least I could do to thank her for taking care of us all those years. You know," he said, "your mother worked hard. There was a time when I thought that women had it easy; all they had to do was housework. How hard could that be? But housework is really hard." He was quiet for a minute then added under his breath as he looked at the old photo, "Especially laundry."

One of the hardest trials we can have in this life is caregiving, whether it is for a whole family or for a loved one who is ill or disabled. If you are caring for someone you love, you may have days when you think you will break. I've had those days too. All I can tell you is this, Christ's love for us enabled him to bear his cross to the end, and that supernatural love will give you the strength to do the same.

Storing Up Treasures in Heaven

Looking Within:

People who love each other serve each other. And yet, in spite of this love, I sometimes feel that the burden is too hard. I forget that sometimes, others find it hard to serve and care for me, too. I know I can do all things in Christ, who strengthens me. I also know that every trial eventually comes to an end, and when it does, I will be at peace if I can look back and say, "I did all I could."

Prayer:

My Jesus, when you fell beneath the weight of your cross it was love that gave you the strength to get up and keep going. I ask you to give me the grace of this great love too so that I may get up and continue to carry my cross in peace and joy.

PART 7

When You Find it Hard to Trust God
Finding Peace in His Promises

CAR TRIBULATIONS
Making Peace When Everything Falls Apart
by Kira Marie McCullough

Have you ever said a Panic Prayer?

I have, many times.

The fearful cries of, "Oh, help us, Lord!" were my common refrain during our car *tribulations* in the summer of 1986.

We were newly married, in love, and expecting our first baby. My growing belly (so cute) added to the bliss of life. I remember driving the winding roads of the Texas heartland, feeling supremely happy as I rode in the car side by side with my beloved, anticipating the birth of our daughter in January of the following year.

August of 1986 marked the fifth month of my pregnancy, and my joy in becoming a new mother seemed boundless—except for the fact that we were dirt poor. My maternity clothes were hand-me-downs from friends. Our bed was a mattress on the floor. There wasn't enough paycheck at the end of the month to even buy a pack of bubblegum. My happiness was often tempered by financial woes and car problems. Most distressing were the car troubles.

Our Datsun B210 hatchback could no longer ferry us reliably. The auto mechanic diagnosed the problem as a rusted drive shaft. The part was not replaceable because it was no longer in production.

"What happens if the drive shaft breaks?" we asked.

"Well," answered the mechanic in a slow Texas drawl seasoned with gravitas, "The car will either stop dead in the road, or..."

Our eyes widened with shock.

Or... y'all will lose control of the steering wheel."

Our faces blanched with panic.

These were terrifying words to a young couple expecting a child and without the means to buy a new car. Thus began a Summer of Panic Prayers.

Panic prayers are emotional cries to God for help, the kind of entreaties that join with the heart of the Psalmist who groans, *Answer me when I call, my saving God. When troubles hem me in, set me free; take pity on me, hear my prayer.* (Psalm 4:2)

Each time I took the wheel of the hatchback, my trust in God was stretched as thin as the metal rod that held our drive train together.

Protect us…Help us, oh Lord! I would pray in desperation.

Every drive across town and back was an exercise in supreme courage. Yet, despite my sweaty hands and palpitating heart, God protected us, until finally, through the generosity of my husband's parents, we were able to buy a newer used car.

When the money arrived in the mail, we gleefully drove to the dealership. We pulled up and while it was still idling, the Datsun B210 shuddered, hacked, and coughed as if in its death throes. Suddenly, we heard an enormous, *clunk!* We got out and looked. Beneath the car, the drive shaft had split in two. We gawked at the rusty-red chunk of metal, a visual of God's faithfulness until the final moment.

Coincidence or Divine Providence?

I believe Divine Providence held our car together, for the timing of our vehicle's demise occurred at the exact moment when we no longer needed it. The Panic Prayers of Summer had reached the ears of our Heavenly Father. He had mercifully quieted our trembling hands on the steering wheel, bringing us peace each time we drove, while at the same time holding together our disintegrating car until the exact right moment.

But the story does not end there.

We bought a big blue boat of a car that day— a Ford Thunderbird, spacious enough for our growing family. Proudly, we drove it off the lot, leaving behind the broken Datsun (our trade-in). We had traveled only a few miles before the gauge on the dash showed an overheating engine. My husband pulled over to the side of the road, as smoke billowed from under the hood. While he turned on the emergency blinkers and hurriedly got out of the car to check the engine, I rushed across the street to a nearby gas station, in hopes that someone would kindly assist us.

"Please, could you help us? Our car is overheating," I asked the attendant standing at the pump.

"We're closing, ma'am," he said coldly, turning his back to me, paying no attention to my pleadings, or the fact that I was almost sixth months pregnant.

Fuming with anger, I stomped back to our car, crying tears of frustration. By this time, with the help of a passing motorist, my husband had pushed the disabled vehicle into a parking lot where it sat like a bedraggled shipwreck.

These were the days before cell phones. We were within a few miles of our house. The only answer was to walk home, despite the muggy heat of the late-August afternoon.

"Take my hand," said my husband, who began leading me down the sidewalk. Along the way, we stopped at a restaurant to eat supper, and after a good meal, we felt well-enough revived to continue the long slog home, stopping frequently so that I could sit and rest my weary pregnant body.

Upon arriving at our little house, my husband called a friend on the phone, and they scheduled a time for him to drop by after work and pick up my husband, with plans to examine the engine of the incapacitated Thunderbird. We were all hopeful that the problem was fixable with a little water and a wrench. It would be midnight before his friend would get off work to pick up my husband, so I went to bed, exhausted.

As I lay in the darkness, I prayed another Panic Prayer. This time, though, my petition comprised a little less panic and a lot more faith. I could see God's hand in the timing of the drive shaft breaking. I could see God's kindness in the walkable distance between our home and the breakdown of the old blue Ford. Surely, God could give my husband and his friend the wisdom to fix it, for we did not have enough money to have it towed to a repair shop.

This scripture came to my mind as I fell asleep,

> *It is vain for you to rise early and put off your rest at night, To eat bread earned by hard toil—all this God gives to his beloved in sleep.*
>
> ~Psalm 127:2

With those verses rolling through my mind, I fell asleep and rested peacefully, without anxiety, without a single Panic Prayer rising to my lips that night. Around 3:00 in the morning, my husband awakened me.

"Good news," he whispered, "I brought the car home! It's in the driveway. We looked it over, checking everything. It was bone dry and needed several quarts of oil. That's all. It should run fine from now on."

With happiness, we bowed our heads in thanksgiving, both exclaiming at the end of our impromptu prayers, "Thank you, Lord."

Our hearts overflowed with gratitude that night, and the Ford Thunderbird became the workhorse vehicle that carried our little family safely, here and there, for years to come.

Our car tribulations became the first of many lessons teaching me the power of prayer—even Panic Prayers—to move the heart and hand of God.

In years to come, Panic Prayers would lead to more trusting prayers of greater faith, as I relied on God's Providence, recognizing that nothing could happen without his permission. I need not fear anything. For the God who feeds the birds of the air could keep a car in motion until the right moment. The God who makes the flowers grow could use the hands of my husband and his friend to fix a car while I slept in peace. The God who hears Panic Prayers will take my worries and fears and give to me sweet rest and deep peace.

Storing Up Treasures in Heaven

Peace comes to us when we give our worries and fears to God. Panic Prayers are the beginning of that trusting relationship. Grow in your confidence and faith by turning your Panic Prayer into a scripture memory verse. Memorize Psalm 127:2 and recite this upon waking, at lunch, and before going to sleep, every day for the next week.

> *It is vain for you to rise early and put off your rest at night, To eat bread earned by hard toil—all this God gives to his beloved in sleep.*
>
> ~Psalm 127:2

Learn What's Normal First
At Peace with Others
by Keb Burns

My mother didn't know it yet, but her life was about to change. Doomed to a few days of boring convalescence in the hospital after surgery, my mother was sitting up in bed, sketching on an artist's pad to pass the time. When her surgeon came by on rounds, he asked to see what she was drawing. Thinking he was just being polite, she thought nothing of it and showed it to him. To her surprise he seemed genuinely interested, so she turned the pages and showed him all the sketches in her pad. She could see the wheels turning in his head as he looked long and hard at each drawing. Suddenly, he said "I've been looking for someone to illustrate a research paper I'm working on. It seems that medical illustrators are pretty scarce around here. Would you be interested in giving it a try?" In the early 1950's, medical photography was not good enough to clearly show the fine details of intricate surgical procedures. At that time, hand-painted illustration was the best way to do this.

My mother was stunned. She stammered, "I'm not a professional artist; I just do this as a hobby. Besides, I don't know anything about medicine!"

He replied cheerily, "That's okay; I don't know anything about art. We'll get along great!"

Then, promising to help her with the medical knowledge she would need, he told her that he would call as soon as she was back on her feet.

True to his word, he called her a few weeks later and asked

her to illustrate an upcoming surgery. She was both thrilled and terrified. She had never seen surgery before and wasn't sure how she would react. On the other hand, this was a dream come true for her. She had long been interested in finding a career in medicine, but with a husband and young children to care for, she never found the time. Nor did she know what specialty to pursue. The idea of combining her interest in medicine with her love of art had never occurred to her; it was a field she had never heard of.

On the day of the surgery, she was too nervous to eat. When she got to the hospital she panicked and started to back out, but just then a nurse came looking for her and led her up to the surgical floor. The nurse showed her how to scrub and put on gloves, gown, mask, and cap. She felt like a child whose mother was dressing her to go outside to play in the snow. Everything felt bulky and clumsy.

When she entered the operating room, she saw that the patient was already anesthetized, and the surgeon and his team were standing around the operating table, waiting for her. The doctor turned and greeted her heartily then pointed to a low stool next to him. "Stand on this and look over my shoulder. I want you to draw it from the same angle I see it." She was feeling queasy and was worried she might faint. Right on cue, the doctor pointed to the corner of the room and said cheerily, "If you're going to faint, do it over there so you won't be in the way."

This embarrassed her and she said firmly, "I am not going to faint!" She swallowed hard and stepped up on the little stool.

"Put your hand on my shoulder so you don't fall," he said.

Again, this pricked her pride, and she retorted "I am not going to fall!"

Nevertheless, she felt unsteady as she juggled the pencils and paper while trying to keep her balance and did have to steady herself on his shoulder once or twice.

The surgeon made the incision, and the body cavity opened up. He chattered a running commentary as he reached his hands into the body, gently pushed aside organs and cut, snipped, and sewed tissue. She put pencil to paper and began sketching but she had no idea what he was doing or what she was looking at. She couldn't tell the difference between healthy tissue and diseased and didn't understand his medical terminology. This, combined with her nausea and the unsteadiness of the stool, made her stop drawing. She realized she was in over her head.

After the surgery, she was devastated that she had failed and embarrassed to have to admit it. "I just didn't know what I was looking at," she told him. Thinking that her medical illustrating career was over before it began, she apologized for letting him down and thanked him for the opportunity. "I'm sorry I couldn't be of more help."

"Hey, you're not quitting on me, are you? Don't quit! This was my fault!" He apologized to her for not preparing her. "Of course you didn't know what you were looking at. I should have realized that. It's just that I know it so well I had forgotten what it's like to be a first-year medical student. Back then, I didn't know what I was looking at either." He told her that he would get her enrolled in anatomy and physiology classes and would get permission for her to access the hospital's private library.

"I'm going to tell you what my mentor told me. Learn what's normal first, then you will automatically recognize what's abnormal. Normal means the way the body is designed to work." The most important skill, he told her, was learning the difference between normal and common. For example, clogged arteries were a common sight; he saw them frequently, but they weren't normal.

"The history of medicine is full of physicians who mistook common for normal," he said. "Whatever we see frequently, we begin to accept and then ignore. Many patients have died because of this. So, learn what's normal first."

Encouraged by his confidence in her, my mother committed herself to learning the human body. She attended classes, built a personal library of medical books, and got permission to watch surgeries and postmortems. She also took classes from a portrait artist who taught her how to draw every bone, muscle, and organ in the human body from memory.

She fell in love with medicine and found joy in how beautifully all the parts of the human body worked together in a well-ordered system. The surgeon was right: by learning the basics well, my mother found that she could spot disorder and disease as soon as she saw it. As she learned, she gained confidence and peace of mind. When he thought she was ready, the surgeon asked her again to draw his surgeries. This time she succeeded. She went on to have a career in medical illustrating, working for doctors in several specialties. Her work was published in medical journals and books. She also became a medical writer, her articles appearing in magazines and newspapers.

My mother found the surgeon's advice applied to many things in life, not just medicine. In fact, she often repeated it to me when I was a child. For example, she would say, "Is it normal for a stranger to walk up to you on the street and offer you candy? Of course not. If that happens, run away and find help." Or she would say, "Do you think it's normal for a friend to lie about you? No? Then maybe she's not your friend." This simple advice taught me to think logically about what was happening around me.

As I grew older, I developed a more spiritual understanding of this concept. I knew whenever anyone tried to normalize the abnormal, I was in the presence of spiritual disease. Just as God designed the human body to work in a particular way, so he also laid out a design for how to live our lives. We can see the original design in the Genesis story of creation, in the Ten Commandments, the Beatitudes, and the parables and sermons of Jesus. All of these passages give us an image of peaceful relationships, rooted in love. God's plan for us is a mirror of Himself

We love because he first loved us.

~1 John 4:19

It's common for today's families, communities, and countries to be at war with each other, as common as clogged arteries, in fact. Because it is so common, we are tempted to think of it as normal. As the surgeon said, whatever is common we begin to accept and then ignore. This leads to death. If we treat conflict in our family as normal, love will die. If we begin to think of war as normal, people will die. This is not God's original design for us. How do we get back to God's original design? By doing what my mother did: study and practice!

First, start reading. Do you know the Ten Commandments by heart? The Beatitudes? Have you read the four Gospels, the story of creation? Learn what's normal first, the right order of things, the plan laid out for us by God as recorded in Scripture, then you can more easily recognize what's abnormal in your own life and in the world around you.

Second, practice, practice, practice. Practice the peace you read about in Scripture. We are designed to be a mirror of God and

> *...he is not the God of disorder but of peace.*
> ~1 Corinthians 14:33

Peace is the original design. Peace is normal.

Storing Up Treasures in Heaven

Looking Within:
The next time I am tempted to insult my spouse, yell at my children, or fight with my neighbors, I will stop and remember, this is not normal. This is not the original design for my life that God gave me.

Prayer:
My Jesus, help me organize my day so that I may make time to read your plan for my life in the Scriptures. Give me the grace to practice the peace you have taught me by your life and your Word.

THE MEEK SHALL INHERIT THE EARTH
Finding Peace in God's Promises for Here and Hereafter
by Kira Marie McCullough

As a child, I was blessed to grow up in a place so enchantingly beautiful that I fell head over heels in love with God's creation. In the summertime, I raced barefoot through the green grass. I climbed to the sky through the branches of lofty pines and descended to the earth to explore cool caverns carved into hidden hillsides.

In 1970, my family moved to this scenic place surrounding a small Ohio town beside a lazy river, nestled in the foothills of the Appalachian Mountains. For a decade we lived there, during my formative years of childhood, into my teens.

Summer was best because there was no school and the weather was nice. After breakfast in the mornings, I would fly outdoors into the sunshine and fresh air for tree-climbing, creek-stomping, or simply moseying through the backyard, plucking honeysuckle flowers from the vine and extracting their delicate stamens to taste the sweet nectar.

Our backyard was a double rolling hill that ended at a tree-lined barbed wire fence, beyond which was Cash's Lot—a square mile of treeless expanse, of rocky earth-turned-mud after rainstorms. Reminiscent of the flatland left behind after strip mining, the broad, brown space sprouted random clusters of prairie grasses and wildflowers after the rain. The plateau stretched away from our house, westward, dipping downwards and disappearing into a series of terraced cliffs. Below these lay a tiny forest with a well-worn trail leading to the road in front of the elementary school that I attended. It was a magical place to be a child.

Since there were no fences between yards, the neighborhood children roamed and played freely. Between our neighbor's house and Cash's Lot was a wide ditch filled with tall, dried grasses, perfect for hiding in. The golden blades packed tightly together, reaching above our heads.

One August morning, my friend, Lanny, and I, decided to build a tunnel made of grass. Flexible enough to bend and curve, the grasses were pliable in our hands, and we twisted and tied them together to form an arch. We spent hours in the warm sunshine weaving the stalks, stamping our way through the middle to produce a level floor.

The result was rather spectacular. We had a created a natural shelter, large enough to hold several children. Satisfied with our work, we sat inside of the tunnel, where the sunlight made crisscrossing patterns on the ground, and we breathed in the fragrance of flower-scented warmth.

Then my mother called me inside to eat lunch. I ate a peanut butter and jelly sandwich with apple slices and potato chips, stuffing my face and chewing fast so that I could get back to our grass tunnel and play.

Suddenly, I heard the sound of shouting outside. Startled, I looked through the kitchen window and my heart burned at the sight. I could see Lanny and several other children jumping up and down and hollering, stamping the grasses of the tunnel with glee. I trembled with rage.

Running through the door, I yelled at them, "Stop! Quit it! *Stop right now!*"

The boys ignored me, continuing their destruction with evil laughter and mockery. Within minutes, the grass house had collapsed into a crunchy pile of straw beneath their tennis shoes.

For the first time in my life, I experienced the feeling of powerlessness in the face of absolute domination and brute force. The other boys had ruined our grass tunnel, but my friend had betrayed me by joining them. I carried this injustice with me for many years.

113

As grownups, we know that despite our best efforts to live at peace with everyone, evil people still exist and wickedness may reign, bringing chaos to our lives like the demolition of my straw shelter. How do we react when our lives are shaken and trampled beneath the feet of scoffers? How do we find peace when it appears as if malevolent men have prevailed?

We begin by remembering the words of Jesus, who reassures us that Good will eventually triumph over Evil. It is his will that the Kingdom of God be established in hearts, homes, and nations. The Kingdom of God—which is righteousness, peace, and joy— will eventually be victorious. His conquest will come not through dominating, tyrannical power, but through the meek and humble hearts of the forgiving.

Blessed are the meek, for they will inherit the land.
~Matthew 5:5

Once upon a time I inherited a couch and a table. Years later, when my grandmother died, I got a packet of sentimental jewelry and linen tablecloths. Physically, I have inherited by mother's nose and my father's sarcastic smile.

But in this bible passage, we are told that we will inherit the Earth. How can that be?

Everywhere, we see evidence of the bullies and despots, who take the world by force, as if they were kings of the globe. Their greed steals the land from farmers, and their quest for power crushes the rights of the poor.

However, the meek receive the gift of the Earth from God, as thankful stewards. Though it does not appear that meekness is winning, one day, it will, and this triumph echoes throughout scripture:

But the earth shall be filled with the knowledge of the Lord's glory, just as the water covers the sea.
~Habakkuk 2:14

The righteous will inherit the earth and dwell in it forever.

~Psalm 37:29

Your people will all be just;
*   for all time they will possess the land;*
They are the shoot that I planted,
*   the work of my hands, that I might be glorified.*

~Isaiah 60:21

These verses give us a glorious glimpse of the "coming of the Kingdom of God," on earth. Like the rising sun on the horizon, the light of God's righteousness, peace and joy will one day illuminate all hearts, spreading from person to person until the entire earth blooms into a new paradise. We can only speculate about how and when this will happen. I am not a theologian. But one thing is certain—scripture suggests a mysterious time of peace, the restoration of all things, coming to the earth for a season. Not by human hands, but by God's decree. Not through false leaders whose smooth ways flatter and deceive—but through the divine intervention of God.

Look Beyond Your Troubles and You Will See God's Blessings

On that day that the straw house was destroyed, I flew into the fray of the wild boys, flailing my arms and screaming at the top of my lungs. Not only had I lost the fruit of my afternoon's labors, but I had lost my temper, my peace, and my vision. If I had only glanced over my shoulder I would have seen, rising like a castle on the hill, our family's sturdy, two-story house. Waiting inside were my loving parents, my precocious sister, and a floor made of gleaming hardwood, rather than packed dirt. Hot meals, entertaining television shows, sudsy baths, clean clothes—all of this awaited inside of those four walls beneath the shingled roof,

115

which had withstood icy winter winds, and fierce spring storms.

Pride in my childish creation outdoors—a fragile shelter—had limited my ability to perceive reality, shadowing my perspective like a beam in my eye. Behind me stood the evidence of my parents' love for me, the work of their hands, fruit of their labors—a house we called home.

When the things we love in this world begin to crumble, totter, and fall, we need to ask God to restore our vision, to see beyond the ruined grass tunnel. By the eyes of faith, we ask God for the patience to await the coming of the Kingdom of God, which is a foretaste of the glories of our true, heavenly home, beyond.

Though we hope and pray for an era of peace here and now, we must never lose sight of our ultimate destination. Christians of other ages keenly understood the concept that this world is not our eternal home. They yearned for Heaven.

> *For here we have no lasting city, but we seek the one that is to come.*
>
> ~Hebrews 13:14

We can rejoice in knowing that this kingdom begins on earth, in our hearts, and extends all the way to Heaven.

Storing Up Treasures in Heaven

Have you been betrayed by a friend? Are you enraged by injustice? Remember God's promise—he wants to give you the Kingdom of God, today and every day. The Kingdom does not belong to bullies, despots, or the proud and arrogant, but rather to the meek and humble.

> *For the kingdom of God is not a matter of food and drink, but of righteousness, peace, and joy in the holy Spirit.*
>
> ~Romans 14:17

Memorize the Lord's Prayer, which Jesus taught us to pray. Make it your goal to commit to memory these words, so that you may voice this life-giving intercession before meals, and spontaneously throughout the day, at moments when you most need peace:

> *Our Father in heaven,*
>   *hallowed be your name,*
> *your kingdom come,*
>   *your will be done,*
> *on earth as in heaven.*
>   *Give us today our daily bread;*
> *and forgive us our debts,*
>   *as we forgive our debtors;*
> *and do not subject us to the final test,*
>   *but deliver us from the evil one.*

~Matthew 6:9–13

Part 8

When you are Suffering
Discovering Peace that Outlasts the Pain

A JOURNEY OF HOPE
Making Peace with Our Past
by Kira Marie McCullough

When I look at my left leg, I see more than flesh covering muscle and bone. I see a nine-inch scar.

Beginning at the midpoint of my thigh and traveling down my leg and around my kneecap is the mark of the surgeon's knife. It is the only visible sign of a horrific car accident that changed my life more than forty years ago.

Yet, the blows that I suffered that night have been softened over time by the tender mercies of God—and today, that thin white line stretching from thigh to knee, curved like a shepherd's staff, reminds me of Psalm 23:

> *Even though I walk through the valley of the shadow of death, I will fear no evil, for you are with me; your rod and your staff comfort me.*
>
> ~Psalm 23:4

Experienced shepherds tell us that when a wandering ewe falls into deep ditches or gets trapped in a tight spot, the shepherd comes along with his staff. He lowers the carved wooden instrument into the depths of a cliffside thicket, or pokes into the grove of brambles, until he can deftly catch the sheep around the belly and retrieve the helpless animal from its dangerous predicament.

The scar in the shape of a shepherd's staff is my daily reminder of the Good Shepherd's rescue from a dangerous situation and his kindness that eventually restored peace and hope. However, this was a process. I had to journey through a lengthy recuperation of both body and soul.

The accident happened during the summer before my sophomore year in college, while I was living at home with my parents in the small town of Kingsville, Texas. A year earlier, I had begun dating a young man from my church, Dennis. We saw one-another weekly at the church youth group and choir. I was nineteen and he was twenty, and we were soon madly in love. I dreamed that one day he would ask me to marry him.

As July approached, Dennis and I volunteered to be counselors for disadvantaged city kids at a church camp in the Hill Country of Texas. On the weekend of the retreat, Dennis drove to my house, picking me up in his family's two-door Chevy. We sped north taking farm-to-market roads to avoid heavy highway traffic. It wasn't long before the sun set, and we found ourselves enveloped in pitch-black darkness.

The Texas countryside at night is like the depths of a dark, yawning cave lit by the flame of a candle or the battery of a flashlight. If you have ever been spelunking, you know what I mean. The farther you go, the wider the expanse, until you realize that you are in a place too vast to see everything within the circle of that tiny light. Traveling through an ebony landscape with only the pin prick of our headlights to guide us, we strained to see more than a few yards beyond our car.

If we had been driving during the daylight, we would have easily seen the thinning of the road and the bridge marker, and would have had enough time to adjust our course. But in the cavernous night, the warning signs appeared too late. Suddenly, the right lane narrowed, and a slightly raised concrete buttress rose before us, indicating we were milliseconds from entering the deck of a short bridge.

We hit the abutment with such force that it blew the right front tire to shreds, causing Dennis to lose control of the steering wheel. It took every ounce of his strength to keep the car steady

121

and straight. He surely realized he needed to veer into the other lane on our left, but he hadn't the time. We found ourselves flying up onto the bridge railing, balancing precariously on the two left wheels. We raced along for a few seconds before the weight of the car tipped to the right.

In a powerful jerking motion, the tires sheared off the railing, sending us plummeting from the edge, into the dry creek bed below.

It seemed as if the entire universe had been suspended at that moment, holding its breath, as the thought flashed through my mind, *I am going to die.* I was flung violently against the passenger door, knocked into a stupor, and though I could feel the motion of rolling end over end across the ground, I was helpless, lost in blackness. Like a rag doll, my body slipped out of my seatbelt and slumped to the floorboard, where I folded into a tight ball, protected from the crushing roof.

Two men in a passing car saw the entire accident. They stopped and ran down the hill, somehow able to pull open the mangled door and release me from the wreckage. I remember slipping into unconsciousness as they dragged me from the car. When I awakened, I looked up into the sky at the moon through eyes streaming with blood from the cuts on my face and head. One of the men raced to a nearby house to call an ambulance while the other remained by my side. Through a liquidy blur, I saw his kind smile and heard the muffling of his words, "Don't be afraid. Help is on the way."

It was only after we had reached the hospital that I learned what had happened to Dennis. He was a tall young man. The impact of the car falling from the bridge and landing on its roof had killed him instantly.

After fifty stitches below my right eye and several x-rays, my parents drove to the hospital to take me home, my body covered with bruises and cuts. Painful as the physical injuries were, nothing hurt more than the realization that I had lost my beloved.

I entered a dark night of the soul, deeply grieving over the loss of my boyfriend. Yet, the pain in my heart masked the pain in my body, for it was only after many days that we discovered deeper injuries needing to be addressed. Although the bruises and lacerations slowly healed over the next few weeks, I was finding it more and more difficult to walk.

In August my parents finally took me to our family physician, who discovered that in a freakish way my thigh muscle had been severed, without the breaking of the skin. When the doctor pressed his hand against my leg, his fingers found a gigantic hollow above my knee. An x-ray confirmed his diagnosis: a bisected quadricep. Emergency surgery was needed to re-attach my thigh muscle.

It is fascinating to me how muscles, bones, and joints work together. We need all three in order to move our bodies, and when one does not work properly, the body suffers.

When all three are working in harmony, there is peace.

God, being the Holy Trinity, has a special affinity for the number three. In the Bible, we read that there are three theological virtues: faith, hope, and love. I consider faith to be like a muscle—it does the heavy lifting. From moving laundry baskets to climbing mountains, we need the strength of muscles. To ascend the spiritual ladder of virtues and grow in holiness, we need the muscle of faith.

Hope is the joint—it smooths the way. We take it for granted, until it is lost. When the cartilage thins so that bone scrapes bones, there is discomfort, and sometimes debilitating pain. The loss of hope cripples us, and our spiritual walk becomes a limp. When I lost Dennis, I lost the dream of one day becoming his bride. My hope had been deferred.

Hope deferred makes the heart sick...
~Proverbs 13:12

Finally, I like to think of Love as the bone—the firm foundation, the strong structure holding everything together. The skeletal bones are the only part of the body that remain after the decay of death. In a similar fashion, Love endures, overcoming all.

Love never fails.

~1 Corinthians 13:8

When all three function harmoniously—muscle, joint, and bone—there is peace within the body. As we make peace with our past, we need the muscle of faith, the ligament of hope, and the rock-solid strength of Love. When these theological virtues work in harmony, our souls are renewed and refreshed, awakening to a future of hope.

After the surgery and many months of physical therapy, I was able to walk again, albeit with a slight limp (which I will always have).

Next, it was time to heal my heart.

I started counseling with a psychologist named Jackie. For the next year, our goal was to obtain greater spiritual, mental, and emotional healing. Weekly, he talked me through my pain, encouraging me to dredge up the memories.

One day he said that it was time for closure. He was going to drive us to the spot where the crash had occurred, three hours to the north of our little town of Kingsville. We set a date on the calendar.

When the day came, we began our journey. It was a surreal experience, riding in a car in bright sunshine, along the same route that Dennis and I had taken two years before in the dark of night.

When we reached the bridge, Jackie parked the car on the gravel feeder road.

We got out and walked down the hill, into the dry creek bed, our legs brushing the pale swishing grasses, our faces shadowed by the leafy branches of the great oaks along the banks. We looked in amazement at the bridge so high above, and I replayed the events of the night out loud to my counselor, sharing for the umpteenth time what had happened.

When I had finished, we were both quiet. We stood across from each other, looking at the channel of grass between us where water should have flowed. Then Jackie said something remarkable and unexpected.

"I see you holding a baby one day in your arms."

Shocked, I looked up from my reverie to stare at him.

"Yes, one day you will be a mother of children, and you will be happy again."

His words brought a strange thrill to my heart, like the dawning sun after a long night of storms. He had restored my hope—hope that what had happened on that shadowy night on a bridge was not the end of my story. It was the beginning.

"Yes, one day you will be a mother of children, and you will be happy again," he repeated.

Jackie's words planted a mustard seed of faith in my heart. After we returned home, I pondered the thought that God had a future and a hope for me, and so I began to pray. Four years later I would meet the man who would become my husband. Through the strength of love, I entered a new life as a wife and happy mother of children.

Just as my story did not end at the bridge, Proverbs 13:12 does not end on a dire note, but continues with a resounding chorus of expectation:

> *Hope deferred makes the heart sick, but a wish fulfilled is a tree of life.*
> ~Proverbs 13:12

I am glad for the doctors who repaired my leg. I am thankful for my counselor, Jackie, and my family and friends who loved me unconditionally through it all. They cried with me and cheered for me as I pressed through the pain, the sadness, and the doubts.

Making peace with our past requires a journey of hope. The car accident was one sudden tragic moment of trauma, but recovery happened through many slow, tiny steps. Though I limped through those steps, I was never alone, for the Good Shepherd was guiding me, restoring my peace.

Storing Up Treasures in Heaven

Do you need to make peace with your past? Though you may remember many hurtful incidents from your life, pick just one. Write your recollection briefly in a journal, using only a few sentences.

Next, pray to Jesus as the Good Shepherd, asking for inner healing, and offer your memory to his Sacred Heart—when you recall the incident at other times, pray, "Jesus, I place this in Your Sacred Heart."

If you become aware of any unforgiveness associated with the painful memory, ask God for the grace to forgive those who have hurt you. Ask the Good Shepherd to guide you to kind-hearted people who can take this journey of hope alongside you. As time goes on, write other memories in your journal and follow the same path of offering it up to the Sacred Heart of Jesus, sharing discretely with trusted friends, and forgiving.

One day, you will arrive at your destination—the glorious grace of a peaceful heart—and you will tear the pages of these written memories from your journal and throw them away, joyously exclaiming, "It is finished!"

> *You have turned my mourning into dancing for me; you have untied my sackcloth and encircled me with joy, that my soul may sing praise to You and not be silent. Lord my God, I will give thanks to you forever.*
>
> ~Psalm 30: 11, 12

ACROSS TIME AND SPACE
At Peace with Suffering

by Keb Burns

It had been three hours since I had returned to my room after my surgery, and I still had not been given any pain medication. There was a six-inch slice in my stomach, which had been stapled together with little bits of metal. I marveled that the human body could endure so much pain and still live. I asked the nurse if I could have pain medication now.

"Not until your vital signs stabilize, dear," she replied sweetly and left the room.

In a few minutes another nurse came into the room and said (not so sweetly) "Time to turn over. You don't want to get fluid in your lungs."

I obeyed, but it was agonizing. And yet, in spite of the suffering, I was supremely happy. Why? Because I had decided to imitate the Apostle Paul. He once wrote something that many people find puzzling but that I understood perfectly and completely identified with. He said:

> *Now I rejoice in my sufferings for your sake, and in my flesh I am filling up what is lacking in the afflictions of Christ on behalf of his body, which is the church.*
> ~Colossians 1:24

Like Paul, I had decided to offer up my suffering to fill up in my flesh what was lacking in the sufferings of Christ on behalf of his church. In fact, I had a few particularly nefarious members of his church in mind I was praying for…but we needn't go there. Like Paul, I was filled with joy, happy to be able to turn my suffering into something useful for God.

This statement of Paul's strikes a lot of people as being odd, maybe even a little heretical. After all, there was nothing lacking in the suffering of Christ, was there? No, it lacked nothing. Christ alone is the one true mediator. Christ didn't need anybody's help to redeem the world. His own efforts were entirely sufficient. So, what was Paul talking about?

Strictly speaking, Jesus didn't save us by his suffering. Suffering has no intrinsic value. Rather, it was the love with which Jesus suffered that saved us, not the suffering itself. After all, Scripture does not say "Suffering covers a multitude of sins." It says, "Love covers a multitude of sins." 1 Peter 4:8. Redemptive suffering is simply a manifestation of the lengths to which love will go for the beloved.

At the Last Supper, on the night before he died, Jesus told the Apostles:

> *I give you a new commandment: love one another. As I have loved you, so you also should love one another.*
> ~John 13:34

Paul had a brilliant insight into this. How can we love one another as he loved us unless we do what he did? Jesus didn't need our help to save the world, rather, he made room for us to help so that we might have the privilege of imitating him. This is part of the dignity he bestowed on us as creatures made in his image and likeness.

Paul understood that in some mysterious way, we can reach across time and space and unite our sufferings as an act of love to the sufferings of Jesus on the cross, so that Jesus can, in turn, offer our suffering to the Eternal Father along with his own. In that way, our suffering gains the power of his love. It doesn't matter that the crucifixion was over 2,000 years ago. God is outside of time and space, and when God accepts our prayers and suffering, they transcend time and space, too.

Storing Up Treasures in Heaven

Looking Within:

I should never seek out suffering, but when it comes my way, my suffering can be infused with great value. I can unite my suffering to that of Jesus on the cross. Covered in the Blood of Christ, my suffering will become a powerful prayer.

Prayer:

My Jesus, so wounded and sorrowful unto death, I unite everything I suffer today, all my physical pains, worries and sorrows to your suffering love. Like you and like Paul, I rejoice in my sufferings because you have given me the privilege of offering them up for those I love.

THE SHEPHERD OF MY HEART
Making Peace through the Prayer of Abandonment
by Kira Marie McCullough

During the months of my pregnancy, I prayed fervently for the safe delivery of our third child, to whom I gave the nickname, "my little lamb." In the Fall of 1995, God answered my prayer for a safe and happy delivery, and we welcomed our daughter, Joy, into our arms, our hearts, and our home.

Born on November 6th, she appeared healthy; however, over the next few days she weakened, becoming frail and lethargic, unresponsive, and unable to nurse. This began a series of exploratory medical tests, of poking and prodding by doctors searching for a cause.

Finally, six days after her birth, Joy underwent major surgery for a bowel obstruction. This led to two weeks of recovery in the hospital, culminating in the surprising diagnosis of a genetic disease: *cystic fibrosis.*

Having never heard of this chronic illness, we asked the specialists, "Will she be able to eat? To walk? To ride a school bus?" They assured us that she would do typical things and appear normal because CF does not affect the growth or maturation of a person. Rather, it is an obstructive disease, blocking the pancreas and filling the lungs. It is undetected except by genetic testing and unseen apart from the coughing and wheezing.

My life as a mother changed drastically—not only because I now had an infant, toddler, and pre-teen to care for, but because of Joy's daily medical therapies. Overnight, I became a rookie nurse. There were multiple rounds of nebulized medications to be administered from morning till day's end, in order to expel excess mucous and fight various infections; there were enzymes to be mixed with applesauce and given by mouth so Joy could digest milk. Weekly, we visited the CF specialists and other doctors. At the time of her birth, the life expectancy for children with CF was thirty-three years of age.

Parenthood is not for the fainthearted

During the first few months after Joy's diagnosis of CF, I poured through the Bible, highlighting passages of Jesus' healing ministry, amazed by examples of the weak and sick who had been restored to health by our Savior's words and touch. My favorite verses were found in the book of John, chapter 9.

> *As he passed by he saw a man blind from birth. His disciples asked him, "Rabbi, who sinned, this man or his parents, that he was born blind?" Jesus answered, "Neither he nor his parents sinned; it is so that the works of God might be made visible through him.*
>
> ~John 9:1–3

Like blindness, there is no known cure for cystic fibrosis. The blind man had been born with an incurable condition, even as Joy had been. Cystic fibrosis is a genetic disease passed to a child through both parents, and those who carry the DNA for this chronic illness have a one-in-four chance of conceiving a child with CF.

Yet Jesus promised the blind man that his malady would glorify God; and so I prayed incessantly for Joy's healing to happen now, in a dramatic fashion, before any more surgeries or illnesses. I demanded her healing, assuming that this would glorify God most. I clung to the hope of what had happened next to the blind man:

*When he had said this, he spat on the ground and made
clay with the saliva, and smeared the clay on his eyes, and
said to him, "Go wash in the Pool of Siloam" (which means
Sent). So he went and washed, and came back able to see.*
~John 9:6, 7

In the winter of 1996, we returned to the hospital for a second
operation, the reversal of Joy's ileostomy (an opening in the abdom-
inal wall that's made during surgery). The surgeon declared that
within three days we would go home because, by then, her intes-
tinal tract should be functioning normally. The sign would be her
first poopy diaper.

Three days following the surgery, we were still in the hospital
with no evidence of success. Altogether, she endured nine days of
torment, being denied food until the bowels were functioning with
only slight relief from pain medication. Watching "my little lamb"
suffer brought greater distress to me and my husband.

The doctor recommended a third surgery, but before that, he
would order one more X-ray. This crucial test would determine
his decision.

I felt crushed by this turn of events. How could such a frail,
sickly child survive a third surgery in four months? I had been
praying ardently. I felt confused by the silence of God. Why had
he not intervened?

I took my baby into my arms, holding her as I seated myself
in the rocking chair of the hospital room. Weeping and praying,
I waited for an orderly to come and take us by wheelchair to the
X-ray department. In the background the television hummed.
Through blurry eyes I looked up and saw the face of a well-known
evangelist on the screen. Fascinated, I listened to her sermon.

"Jesus is the Lamb of God," she said. "For love of the Father,
and for us, Jesus willingly laid down his life, dying on the Cross.
He was the perfect, unblemished offering of the Father, who gave
His Son so that we might be reconciled to God by the shedding

of His Blood." Then the evangelist asked an intriguing and met-aphorical question:

"What are you willing to offer to the Father out of sheer love? Do you have a lamb to give to God?"

I glanced down at the face of my child, twisted with pain, her little body squirming in my arms. I thought of her nickname, "my little lamb." I thought of Mary, who had embraced the blessings of motherhood, giving her *fiat* to God when the Angel announced that she would conceive by the Holy Spirit. Thirty-three years later she would be called to endure the unique sorrows of stand-ing beneath the Cross, watching Jesus suffer and die as he offered himself for the salvation of all mankind.

Was I willing to quit my wrestling match with God and surrender the future—willing to accept anything—whether my child died before her first birthday, or lived a long life with chronic illness? Did I have the strength of will, the humility of heart, to offer my littlest lamb to the Father, whether or not she was healed today—tomorrow—or in the distant future?

With a gigantic sigh, I entered into a profound prayer of aban-donment. All of the months of resisting the diagnosis, of pleading for her healing, were replaced with unconditional surrender. In tears, I gave Joy to God—and suddenly, all worry, fear, and pain vanished. My soul was instantly restored to the "peace that passes all understanding" (Phil. 4:7–9).

I was at peace, whether she lived or died, because I had been endued with the grace of assurance. A supernatural *knowing* had entered my heart, reassuring me that "my little lamb" was safe in the hands of the Good Shepherd.

The orderly came through the door at that moment. He set-tled us in a wheelchair, took us down the hall until we reached the X-ray department. After donning the obligatory lead apron, I stood beside the enormous radiation equipment where my daughter had been placed on the table. When the technician removed her diaper to prepare for a barium enema, we were greeted with the

133

most amazing sight—something every mother of a newborn sees daily, but for me, was the first time: *A stinky brown mess of poo!* It was the sign that her intestines were working. I jumped up and down in my heavy, lead-lined apron shouting, "Praise the Lord!"

The third surgery was canceled, and within days, we were happily reunited with the rest of the family at home. Yet, my journey did not end there. I still had a mission ahead of me: to keep my child as healthy as possible, and to believe the promises of God for "my little lamb"—promises that included his loving presence, his bountiful mercy, and even his amazing miracles.

Mary's journey did not end at the Cross, either, for she knew that her Son was destined for great things. She remembered what the Angel had told her in the beginning:

> *Behold, you will conceive in your womb and bear a son, and you shall name him Jesus. He will be great and will be called Son of the Most High, and the Lord God will give him the throne of David his father, and he will rule over the house of Jacob forever, and of his kingdom there will be no end.*
> ~Luke 1:31–33

Though I would never again presumptuously demand miracles from God, I would meekly and gently (with a bit of a nudge and sense of humor) remind him of his promises. I learned how to be more trusting, yet still fervent with my Heavenly Father—just like a child tugs the shirt sleeve of his Daddy, saying, "Remember, Daddy, you promised me an ice-cream cone after the doctor's visit!" The scripture about the blind man became God's personal message of love for my daughter. Without panic or despair, I clung lightly, not tightly, to the hope of Joy's eventual healing. As I exercised the tiny mustard seed of faith, the belief grew in my heart that one day, God would do for Joy what was impossible for modern medicine.

In the meantime, I had to let go of the pain—the shock of the diagnosis, the trauma of those early surgeries, the initial fear and anxiety—in order to live more fruitfully in each present moment. Over the years, the love of God became a template for our lives, through all of Joy's illnesses, recoveries, and surgeries, interspersed with the beautiful times of respite when we managed to rise above the disease and live gloriously.

Today, Joy is a beautiful twenty-nine-year-old wife, and the doting mother of two little boys. I continue to pray for her healing, hopeful that her story will resolve like that of the blind man's. In the meantime, I am thankful for the life she is living and the lessons I am learning as her mother.

I was tested to my limit after Joy's birth, but by God's grace, was given the key to peace—the prayer of abandonment. There have been many other prayers of abandonment that I have offered for all of my children, and many other opportunities to face new fears and worries as a mother. The tests that we take and master in our spiritual lives often become ongoing mini-lessons that we must review over and over again. This is why we must make peace with our past, and receive the gift God is offering by letting go— otherwise, we consign ourselves to living the negative memories over and over again in our minds, emotions, and choices.

Storing Up Treasures in Heaven

Is there a past trauma that is keeping you in emotional pain? Ask God for the grace to *let go* of the memories that bind you. Daily for the next week, meditate on this scripture, saying each line slowly and thoughtfully, imagining that God is speaking directly to you in your situation.

> *Do not fear: I am with you;*
> *do not be anxious: I am your God.*
> *I will strengthen you, I will help you,*
> *I will uphold you with my victorious right hand.*
> ~Isaiah 41:10

PART 9

When You Want to Know God Better
Finding Peace with the One Who Knows You Best

THE THREE R'S
Creating Peace Through Prayer
by Kira Marie McCullough

From the time I could walk under the table as a three-year-old to the grown-up days of mothering my own toddlers, the TV set has had the distinction of being positioned in a prominent place in our family home. The house was filled with the yacking of talk show hosts grilling guests on salacious topics, or the earsplitting screams of frenetic crowds cheering their favorite teams to victory in football stadiums.

Today, I get my news and entertainment mostly from my lap-top computer, and as a result, my home has become more like a quiet solitude—less noisy. However, when I discovered the free internet channel—YouTube—I was suddenly hooked on a different kind of distraction. Instead of hundreds of TV channels to choose from, I had tens of thousands of videos to peruse. The gatekeepers of Google make their own recommendations, and often these suggested webcasts show up unannounced and unsolicited. Recently, I made a list of a few of the options they showcased:

- *Dangerous asteroids plummet towards earth*
- *Super cellular tornadic outbreaks ruin lives in the Midwest*
- *Sightings of aliens rattle residents of the West Coast*

My human tendency is to become entangled by the tragedies unfolding around me. Like a moth drawn to a lightbulb, I flitter towards the bad news. Yet, another urge battles for pre-eminence: the desire for the true, the good, and the beautiful.

This desire is satiated by the simple and sweet visuals of hearth and home appearing side by side with the webcasts of fires, earthquakes, and dire predictions of the end of the world. There is the asteroid, next to a video of a goofy teenager strumming banjo tunes to her clucking chickens. Below, a webcast screams, "Danger!" while above, a quaint Irish woman whispers the recipe for dandelion jelly. Choosing to watch the less exciting videos, my blood pressure goes down, my heart rate normalizes, and I can actually fall asleep.

Our lives could be likened to a YouTube feed. Daily, we are presented with choices. Will we choose the terrifying or the comforting, the sensational or the serene?

Scripture encourages us to choose the latter:

> *Finally, brothers, whatever is true, whatever is honorable, whatever is just, whatever is pure, whatever is lovely, whatever is gracious, if there is any excellence and if there is anything worthy of praise, think about these things.*
> ~Philippians 4:8

Our hunger for the true, the good, and the beautiful needs to be satisfied in virtuous ways or we will lose our peace. How do we *center our mind* on what is pure, and *implant in our hearts* that which is honorable, excellent and praiseworthy? I have found that I am happiest when I follow the lead of our Savior, who often awakened early in the morning to pray.

> *Rising very early before dawn, he left and went off to a deserted place, where he prayed.*
> ~Mark 1:35

What is prayer? There are as many versions as there are people. But my simple definition is this:

Talking to God

We can do this anywhere, at any time: In the car; while washing dishes; outside in the garden or while walking the dog; or even at 3 a.m. when insomnia steals our sleep. Whether we speak silently in our minds or give rise to our thoughts vocally, any conversation that we might have with another person, we can have with God.

Our chat can be short and sweet, like a text on the phone, or lengthy and rambling, like a leisurely discussion during breakfast.

While it is a good thing to have a running discourse throughout the day or at certain moments as we go about our tasks, it is also important to dedicate a time and space for more intimate and quiet prayer. Whether this works best for you in the mornings, middays, or afternoons depends on your lifestyle and circumstances. Regardless, we can take our cue from Jesus, who took time to be with the Heavenly Father without interruption.

> *But he would withdraw to deserted places to pray.*
> ~Luke 5:16

For me, mornings are best. As the sun rises, you will find me peacefully propped against my pillows on the bed, surrounded by devotional books, my favorite Bible, my journal, ink pens, and a jar of colorful pencils. I call this my *quiet time*. I pray, read scripture, and write about the verses I am reading. In my diary, I notate the spiritual insights I glean from the Bible and the ongoing personal requests in my heart, adding the answers to my prayers when they come.

This habit of praying daily has not been quickly, nor easily, formed. My earliest attempts to set aside regular quiet time, as a younger woman in my twenties, were not always successful. My mind wandered to the chores, the grocery list, and the piles of paperwork on the desk. Prayer was interrupted by crying babies or toddlers fussing for breakfast. But over the years, I have learned to minimize the distractions by rising earlier than the rest of my family.

Today, the morning prayer and devotions have lengthened from a mere fifteen minutes to an hour (often more) becoming sweeter and more delightful. I think of my superlative times of prayer as if I were having coffee and sweet cake with my best friend. I am sharing my heart and mind freely, learning to *listen* as much as I speak.

I believe that my dedication to this practice of prayer has been one of the main weapons against fear in these troubled times and a powerful pathway to daily peace.

Would you like to know my secret?

Finding peace through prayer requires three things:

- Routine
- Resolve
- Repetition

Routine

Begin small, and grow bigger. In the beginning of my quiet time experiment, I could not focus long on prayer, so I set the timer for fifteen minutes each morning. That expanded to thirty, and then sixty. When a busy list of tasks awaits, I am even more diligent to keep my appointment with God. When my thoughts wander, I try to bring them back to the scripture. I have slowly trained my mind to be more focused.

Yet, I am ever aware that those interruptive feelings and thoughts might be inspirations from God, who is gently leading me in the conversation towards a resolution of my deepest problems. Perhaps, I need to change direction, and intercede for the person who comes to mind; maybe, through my emotions, God is calling me to let go of my anger, fear, or pain; often, he is using my strong emotions to nudge me towards dropping everything I am doing and forgive another person, from my heart.

Every day with God is fresh and new; think of your daily appointment as an opportunity to meet with a friend who loves you so much that he is ecstatic to see you show up each day to meet with him (even in your bathrobe and before brushing your teeth!).

Resolve

This is the persistence and fortitude that keeps us on the couch with our Bibles as the sun rises and the children sleep. I will admit that I don't always enjoy my morning quiet time. Occasionally, I am tired. I experience dryness of spirit. In those moments, I have learned that God is not absent, even if I am. And he wants to be with me even more than I want to be with him. Just showing up at the kitchen table or the front porch rocking chair (or wherever I have chosen to have my quiet time) is enough on those days. I may just sit idly with the Bible on my lap, listening to the birds. But at least I showed up.

The beautiful discovery I have made during spiritual deserts or physical weariness is this: If I persevere, the Lord will bestow once again the times of refreshing.

> *Let us not grow tired of doing good, for in due time we shall reap our harvest, if we do not give up.*
>
> ~Galatians 6:9

Repetition

What is the difference between routine and repetition? Routine is the establishment of a schedule, the development of a daily habit. We make an appointment with God and keep it. But repetition is *the practice of prayer.*

The Bible has been the centerpiece of my prayer adventure through the years. Therefore, some of my favorite prayers come directly from scripture, particularly the Psalms. Any of the 150 Psalms can be turned into a prayer by simply reading the passage aloud, while imagining yourself in the center of the story. Often, I insert my own request between the lines.

There are also ancient and modern devotions in the history of Christendom; these are called chaplets or novenas. Some of these meditate on the mysteries of Christ's life, death, and resurrection, while others may focus on a particular attribute of God, such as his Mercy. And there are many good prayer books that can guide you through daily pre-written reflections.

Repetition does not mean monotony. Prayer is more than words—it is the meeting of two hearts, yours and God's. Prayer is alive and real, because it is a conversation; prayer is vibrant, refreshing, and as varied as a lovely garden of flowers, changing through the seasons. Occasionally, our prayers may seem as brittle as the grass in winter, but these are times when we need God the most. Prayer includes silent tears streaming down our faces, for God hears the words we cannot utter.

> *My wanderings you have noted;*
>   *are my tears not stored in your flask,*
> *recorded in your book?*
>
> ~Psalm 56:9

It is also the joyous cry of our hearts as we sing praises to our God.

> *My soul yearns and pines*
>   *for the courts of the Lord.*
> *My heart and flesh cry out*
>   *for the living God.*
>
> ~Psalm 84:3

Let's recap. What is Prayer? Prayer is simply talking to God. What is the purpose of Prayer? To have an intimate relationship with God, who has designed you and I to love him with all our heart, mind, soul, and strength.

This yearning for the true, the good, and the beautiful needs to be fed through prayer, or we will lose our peace. Technology can distract us, launching us into a frenzy of worry and fear. Daily newscasts can rattle the sensibilities of the most staid. But if we step away from our phone, computers, and TVs, long enough to pray, we will find the peace that surpasses all understanding.

> *Have no anxiety at all, but in everything, by prayer and petition, with thanksgiving, make your requests known to God.*
>
> ~Philippians 4:6

Storing Up Treasures in Heaven

This week, initiate a new habit of prayer. Start by planning a time to meet, uninterrupted, with God—at least once during the day, whatever time is most convenient for you. Then, have your Bible and a journal with pens handy. Set the timer for fifteen minutes, and read one Psalm from the Old Testament and one short chapter from the Gospels (Matthew, Mark, Luke, or John). Silently reflect on the words you are reading. Talk to God honestly about your needs. Then, quietly wait, trusting that he will direct your heart and give you peace.

> *Your word is a lamp to my feet, and a light to my path.*
> ~Psalm 119:105

BEAUTIFUL STRANGER
At Peace with Silence

by Keb Burns

My siblings and I, along with our mother, were gathered around a conference table at the funeral home, consulting with the funeral director, after the sudden death of our oldest brother. In addition to our grief, we had the stress of figuring out how we were going to pay for his funeral. None of us, especially my deceased brother, had been expecting death to come so soon, so no funds had been set aside for this. Each of us had been pouring over our respective bank accounts to see what we could contribute, and it wasn't enough.

I noticed that the funeral director had a slight smile on his face, which I thought was odd. It wasn't a fake, professional smile but soft and kindly. Was that a twinkle I saw in his eye? He presented us with the invoice and asked if there was anything else we wanted to add to the service. We passed it around, glanced at each other with stricken faces and slowly shook our heads no. Then he broke into a full grin and said, "Good. I have been instructed to tell the family that this bill is paid in full. A certain group of people have pooled their money and paid for the funeral. However, there is one condition: I was asked to promise that I would never reveal their identities."

After a long, stunned silence, we all started talking at once. Who could it be? Maybe it was this group. No, it couldn't be them. Maybe it was those people. No, surely not. Who was it? Then we began asking whether or not we could accept such a gift? Isn't it our responsibility to take care of our own family? Finally, my brother Jeb brought some common sense into the discussion.

145

"This is not about us," he said. "This is a gift to Peb (the family nickname for my brother) from his friends. Whoever this group is, they want to honor him. We should not get in the way."

The funeral director asked, "Are you decided then? Shall we go ahead?" We all nodded in agreement.

Then he added, "In all my years in this business, I've never had anything like this happen before. I can tell you this much: these people thought very highly of your brother. He must have been quite a guy."

While I was astonished at the time, later I realized it wasn't surprising at all. My brother was well-loved by many people, even though he was an introvert who spoke little and rarely shared his inner feelings.

Taciturn people are often not well-liked. They can come across as distant at best and hostile at worst. My brother's silence, however, was of a different sort. His silence did not push people away; it drew them in. He was very much engaged as an active listener. He would put down what he was doing, look you in the eye, and listen to every word. Then you could see the wheels turning in his head as he thought about what you told him.

His verbal response may have been sparse, but his actions certainly weren't. A toy would be delivered to a child who was in the hospital, a plane ticket would arrive in the mailbox for someone needing to attend a funeral, money would be slipped under the door for rent, all anonymously. He didn't want anyone to know who did these things because he was humble. It was a fitting tribute that my brother's funeral was paid for anonymously as it's exactly the sort of thing he did for many others. I'm certain he was pleased…and amused.

Oddly enough, I think about my brother when people tell me they don't pray. They give all sorts of reasons: they are too busy, they don't know how, or God already knows what they need, so they don't bother. I'm not sure these excuses are true. I suspect the real reason people don't pray is that they are uncomfortable talking to someone who doesn't talk back. Silence feels like rejection…or worse, indifference. Unfortunately, they misunderstand what's going on. God isn't silent because he is indifferent, he is silent because he is like my brother: listening, thinking, planning some action, and believe it or not, humble. God isn't like a bombastic friend who yells at us from across the room or the chatty friend who loves to talk. He is a Beautiful Stranger who reveals himself little by little. He's a quiet friend who comes from behind and gently takes our arm. While movie-makers love the drama of a God who speaks with thunder and lightning (usually in a British accent), we see from Scripture that God speaks quietly.

In 1 Kings, chapter 19, Elijah the prophet was hiding in a cave in the wilderness from those seeking to take his life. He heard a voice telling him to go out of the cave and stand on the mountainside because the Lord was going to speak to him.

> *There was a strong and violent wind rending the mountains and crushing rocks before the Lord—but the Lord was not in the wind; after the wind, an earthquake—but the Lord was not in the earthquake; after the earthquake, fire—but the Lord was not in the fire; after the fire, a light silent sound. When he heard this, Elijah hid his face in his cloak and went out and stood at the entrance of the cave.*
> ~1 Kings 19:11–13

All of God's attributes are infinite. He is infinite in love, infinite in power, infinite in knowledge. He is also infinite in humility. It was this infinite humility that led him to lower himself to become man, to live a simple life in Nazareth, and to subject himself to torture and death for us. The pinnacle of his work of salvation was done in silence. It is his way.

> *Though harshly treated, he submitted and did not open his mouth;*

147

Like a lamb led to slaughter
or a sheep silent before shearers,
he did not open his mouth.

~Isaiah 53:7

There is another reason God is silent when we pray. God is a higher form of being than you and I. We need words to communicate, but he doesn't. He speaks directly to our souls using the language of grace. Grace doesn't talk, but it does communicate, with an emphasis on *commune.*

Grace opens your mind to knowledge. By grace, you begin to understand things about God you never understood before. Grace opens your mind to understanding yourself better, too. St. Augustine said the reason we can't understand ourselves is that we are made in the image of a God we can't understand. As grace pulls back the veil that obscures the burning light of God, it inevitably illuminates who we are, as well. With habitual prayer, this illumination increases over time.

If you want to find peace and joy in prayer, try this: at least once a week, find a quiet place where you will not be interrupted or distracted. Calm your mind and dive into the silence. At this time, you are not going to ask for any favors or present any needs or worries; save your petitions for another time. Instead, you are going to spend the next half-hour getting to know this Beautiful Stranger. Each time you pray this way, you will realize that you know God a little better than you did before, and you will understand yourself a little better, too. Later, much to your delight, you will find that God has quietly slipped a needed grace into your soul, just as my brother would slip rent money under someone's door.

Storing Up Treasures in Heaven

Looking Within:
When I pray, I will not listen for words, either in my ears or

in my mind. Instead, I will listen for an increase in understanding, an increase in union, an increase in peace. I know that Divine Silence is not empty, it is filled with Grace.

Prayer:

My Jesus, who are you? I want to get to know you better. What makes you happy? What makes you sad? What do you think about as you look upon the galaxies, or a tiny caterpillar…or me? Why did you create the world? Why did you create me? What did you pray about when you were in the desert? What was it like for you to leave Heaven and come to earth and share in our lives? Show me your heart, Lord. Tell me all about yourself. I want to know you better."

As the World Turns Upside Down
Finding Peace through Divine Providence
by Kira Marie McCullough

It was the middle of the night. I had awakened thirsty, needing a glass of water, which was not unusual. What happened next was not only strange, but bizarre. As I swung my legs over the side of the bed, a weird wave of dizziness assailed me. Though my feet had been planted on the ground, my head continued to spin. I buzzed with a strange sensation, reminding me of the shaky feeling of jumping off a revolving merry-go-round on the school playground when I was a child.

Taking my first steps, I almost fell down. Stumbling, I grabbed for the nightside table to regain my balance. Max, my Tabby, leapt from his crouched position nearby, and snatched the edge of my cotton night pants in his mouth; he pulled hard, trying to keep me upright.

Somehow, with my cat shadowing me, I managed to make it to the kitchen for a glass of water by balancing against walls, doors, and furniture. Shaking with fear, I filled the cup with water and unsteadily made a slow and careful journey back to my bedroom. Lowering my head on the pillow, the light-headedness continued, making the darkened room seem to swirl like an emerging solar system cycling into existence. Nothing moved faster, though, than my beating heart, reacting to my emotional panic and anxiety.

I wondered:

Am I dying?

Should I call an ambulance?

I did not hear an audible voice, but I clearly received the

answer to my panicky questions. Softly, like the distant ringing of church bells, these words chimed over and over in my mind: *Fear not.*

In the black night of sickness, I put my trust in those two little words, *Fear not*—because forty years of walking with God had proven to me that he answers even my smallest cries. My breathing slowed, my body relaxed, and I fell asleep to the gentle rhythm of imaginary waves rocking a boat.

The next day, I cautiously drove to the medical clinic. An examination by my doctor netted the diagnosis of benign paroxysmal vertigo—something without a known cause or cure. All she could do was prescribe allergy medication (which I loathe to take, preferring more natural methods of healing when possible). She also gave me a printout of some interesting exercises for the neck and head, assuring me that these movements would lessen the intensity of the annoying occurrences. I faithfully performed these exercises daily, which eased the symptoms, but did not eliminate the vertigo completely.

Little did I know that this malady would come and go, afflicting me for the next three years. The vertigo would hang on for weeks, then disappear, only to return again a few months later. This disorder would show up five distinct times, like an unwelcome guest at the door, disturbing my balance, making certain activities more dizzying than others, usually putting me to bed for the first twenty-four hours.

Over time, I acquired skills of adapting to and controlling the physical symptoms of vertigo through exercise, chiropractic care, and vitamins. I learned to manage the dizzy episodes, getting up to go to work and even driving the car with ease. I learned to accept, on an emotional level, the randomness of this malady, and though I never enjoyed the experience, I stopped fighting its unpredictability.

Most importantly, I grew more dependent upon God; my prayer life was enriched and strengthened. In fact, God took that frustrating illness and turned into a beautiful lesson. Vertigo brought me to a deep, resolute, rich understanding of the Providence of God, which could be described as:

The wisdom of God in ordering the events in the lives of his children for their sanctification and his glory.

Divine Providence is the beautiful and mysterious image of an All-Loving and All-Powerful God, gently stamped into our lives, imprinted upon our very existence. It is the invitation to welcome all things as being permitted by him.

However, this is most difficult to accept when bad things occur. When tragedy strikes, we ask, "Why did God allow this?"

The human mind has devised many answers to this question. There is a strand of belief that insists that God is either *all loving* or *all-powerful*, but could never be both. Such a perspective of God's lop-sided power may lead one to reject God because he appears as a dictatorial tyrant, indiscriminately permitting evil in our lives; on the other hand, believing only in God's love—rendering him devoid of real power to change things—turns him into a weakened comforter, smiling benevolently as we captain our sinking ship to the bottom of the stormy sea.

Additionally, either theological extreme impacts how we view our relationship to God. The *All-Powerful* side of the coin engenders a fatalistic view, stripping us of freewill, causing us to tremble before God as fearful victims; whereas only focusing on the *All-Loving* perspective of God exalts freewill to an almost godlike level—without a powerful God to protect, guide, and heal us, we must rely completely on our own wits and wisdom. These imbalanced perceptions of Divine Providence unsteady us.

A true understanding of Divine Providence reassures us that God loves us tenderly while guiding us firmly, yet always with respect for our freewill. The purpose of Divine Providence is our sanctification and God's glory.

What is sanctification? It is our response to the grace of God. It is a habitual pattern of growth through which God enables us to perfect our souls and to act in charity. The verb *sanctify* derives from the Latin word *sanctifico*, which is rooted in two words: *sanctus*, holy, and *facio*, to make. Sanctification is the process of being made holy. To do this, we must cooperate with God, day by day, by purging all that would keep us from living a virtuous, loving life.

> *If anyone cleanses himself of these things, he will be a vessel for lofty use, dedicated, beneficial to the master of the house, ready for every good work.*
>
> ~2 Timothy 2:21

Divine Providence also calls us to glorify God. How do we glorify God through our illnesses, pains, and difficulties? We glorify him when—like a magnifying glass—we enlarge God in the midst of our smallness and weakness.

> *And Mary said:*
> *"My soul proclaims the greatness of the Lord; my spirit rejoices in God my savior.*
>
> ~Luke 1:46, 47

To carry Christ in our hearts like Mary carried Christ in her womb, requires humility—a mysterious combination of surrender and valor. Mary humbly accepted the Father's invitation to conceive and bear Jesus, the Son of God, when she answered the Angel, *Behold, the handmaid of God. May it be done unto me according to thy will (Luke 1:38)*. Thirty-three years later, she exhibited heroic courage when she stood, unflinchingly, below the Cross, beholding her Son die.

Abandoning ourselves to the will of God while being brave is not easy. For three years, I prayed for relief from vertigo. Every new episode of dizziness sent a shockwave of fear through my being, yet each anxious reaction lessened, and my peace was restored more quickly each time. God was glorified as I clung to the words I had heard from the Lord during the first dark night: *Fear not!* God's power was exalted in my determination to lead a normal life of going to work, shopping, and enjoying friends and family—despite vertigo. In my sickness, I was being sanctified through both surrender and valor.

At the time that I am writing this, I have been vertigo-free for over two years. My prayers for relief have been answered, but beyond than that, my depth of trust in God has been expanded. I have discarded my superstitious belief that there are things out there more powerful than God. I have rejected my fears that I am unlovable. Little by little, day by day, I am learning to trust him more.

This is why my lesson in Divine Providence is a template for "Making Peace in the Present." Facing uncertain times, you and I are called daily to continue this journey of faith, trusting God in every trial and tribulation, putting our confidence in Divine Providence.

When grocery store prices go down, then up again—*Fear not.*
When snow storms block the roads—*Fear not.*
When the electricity is knocked out by high winds—*Fear not.*
Knowledge of Divine Providence gives us balance. Embracing Divine Providence brings us peace. His tender comfort soothes our agitated hearts, while his power overcomes all of our fears, infusing us with the courage to pray and act. Endued by the grace of humility, we wait with patience for his answers.

Storing Up Treasures in Heaven

Today, bring your most troubling situation to God in prayer. Ask him to reveal his purpose in your circumstance. Find a trusted friend, pastor, priest or counselor and share with them your difficult situation, asking for their counsel and wisdom to find God's will in your afflictions. Seek to understand how Divine Providence is bringing about your holiness and his glory. Perhaps, you are in need of developing the virtue of patience, or charity, our courage.

Realize that every trial is an opportunity to draw closer to God in trust, allowing him to guide you as you learn new spiritual skills (this is called sanctification). Meditate on this scripture:

> *We know that all things work for good for those who love God, who are called according to his purpose.*
> ~Romans 8:28

You Still Have to Obey Me
The Peace of Perfect Trust

by Keb Burns

My mother and I were having lunch together at a nice restaurant when we witnessed a preschooler having a meltdown at a nearby table. The little girl was loudly demanding ice cream, and the mother was calmly replying no. After several rounds of this, the little girl burst into angry tears and yelled at her mother, "I hate you!" A look of shock briefly crossed the mother's face, but she remained firm. The child finally gave up and lowered her head in a defeated pout. While the child wasn't looking, I saw the mom turn aside and wipe away tears.

My mother and I were riveted by this drama. When the storm was over, Mom turned to me and said, "You said that to me once."

Astonished, I replied, "Yes, I remember it."

"You remember that?" It was her turn to be astonished.

"Yes, and I remember the answer you gave me. It made a big impression on me. It was very wise."

When I was a preschooler, I found myself in the throes of a similar temper tantrum. Though I was long past the terrible twos, on that particular day I had heard "No" one too many times, and my frustration boiled over.

My body wasn't the only thing that was growing; my mind was also beginning to soar. If my brothers could get on a bus and go to school, why couldn't I? My parents could just walk out the door whenever they wanted to; why couldn't I just walk out the door and go wherever I wanted to go? I watched the mailman out the window and saw him going from house to house. What was in that bag he was carrying? I wanted to go ask him. How did that bird fly from treetop to treetop? If I climbed into that tree, could I fly, too? What's in the alley? Where is that cat going?

Home had always been full of fun things to do, but now curiosity about the outside world had rendered the comfortable and familiar world of home into something small and boring. I was bursting to get out of the house and explore, all by myself, without having to hold an adult's hand or listen to endless warnings like "Don't step in that puddle" or "Don't pet that dog." Normally, my mother could reason with me, but today none of the explanations she gave were sufficient. I didn't want to hear "You're too little. It's not safe. You can when you're older."

I was a prisoner, and my mother was the cruel jailer. Screaming and crying didn't work. Throwing things didn't work. So, I did the most powerful, violent, utterly rebellious thing I could think of. I shouted at her with all the pent-up frustration in my soul, "I hate you!" In my mind, those words tore the bond between us and set me free.

I expected that she would become angry and instant punishment would follow for such a disrespectful outburst. To my surprise, her face softened into a slight smile, and she looked off into the distance for a moment. She was thinking about something far away.

Squatting down to my level, she took my hands in hers and said gently, "That's okay. You can hate me. You are entitled to your feelings..." then in a firm but kindly tone of voice tinged with a bit of sadness, she said, "...but you still have to obey me."

Suddenly, all the fight went out of me. Giving me permission to hate her took all of the extortionary power out of my words. But more than that, her sad, kindly tone of voice made me think that maybe she wasn't trying to dominate me; she was trying to help me. Her standing firm made me see something I had not seen before. No matter what the provocation, no matter what the threat or how cruel the extortion, no matter how violent the storm, she would not, under any circumstances, risk my safety by letting

157

me run around the neighborhood alone. Not even my own hatred could break her resolve to protect me. I knew I was safe as long as I obeyed her. More than that, I perceived something that I had no words for at the time: unconditional love. Peace returned to my soul.

My mother's laugh pulled me back into the present moment. I was no longer a rebellious little girl facing off with a struggling young mother but a grown woman sitting in a restaurant across from my elderly mom. She was smiling at me.

"Well, I wish I could take credit for it," she said, "but I was just repeating to you what my mother told me when I had a temper tantrum at about the same age. Those words made a big impression on me, too. My mother was very wise. She made me feel safe."

"Yes, it had the same effect on me."

My mom sighed, "I'm so glad to hear that. I remembered how angry and frustrated I felt when I was little, so I understood you, and I felt sorry for you. My mother's words helped me, I hoped they would help you, too."

Whenever I think back on this memory, a scripture passage comes to my mind. Saul, the fierce enforcer of the Law, was on his way to the city of Damascus to root out the new heresy called Christianity. He would have done so violently, with prison and death for obstinate offenders. On the way, a mysterious force struck him and his men off their horses. A voice spoke to Paul from out of a blinding light.

> We all fell to the ground, and I heard a voice saying to me in Hebrew, 'Saul, Saul, why are you persecuting me? It is hard for you to kick against the goad.' And I said, 'Who are you, sir?' And the Lord replied, 'I am Jesus whom you are persecuting.'
>
> ~Acts 26:14, 15

What did Jesus mean when he said, "It is hard for you to kick against the goad"? A goad is any kind of instrument that is used to prod horses and cattle in a certain direction. For example, cowboys use spurs, jockeys use little leather whips. A goad could be a simple stick or even one's hand. When an animal wants to go his own way, he will kick against the goad. A compassionate owner will understand the animal's feelings and teach him gently but firmly how to go in the right direction.

Jesus' words "It is hard for you to kick against the goad" suggests to me that God had been inspiring Saul for some time to stop persecuting the followers of Jesus, but Saul had been resisting it. There was such compassion for Saul in this simple statement. Saul had been persecuting Jesus, yet Jesus still had unconditional love for him, while at the same time firmly setting a standard of love for Paul to follow in return. Every time I read this passage, in my mind I hear Jesus speaking to Saul in the same firm, compassionate, but hurt tone of voice my mother used when she said "That's okay. You can hate me…but you still have to obey me."

Looking across the room to the young mother, who was still wiping her eyes from time to time, I realized that my hateful words must have hurt my mother, and her words must have hurt her mother, too. How extraordinary that all three mothers in this story hid their own pain for the sake of love, and how clueless we were as children for not seeing the pain we were inflicting. We had to grow up to see it.

Just as our bodies and minds grow and mature, so too do our souls grow and mature. We have to grow up spiritually to realize that it hurts God as much as it does us when we kick against the goad. Whatever direction he nudges us in is for our good. If we truly believe he loves us, we will trust him. This is more than spiritual maturity, this is relationship.

Storing Up Treasures in Heaven

Looking Within:
    Today, I will trust the boundaries that God sets for me because

I know he loves me and wants only my peace and happiness. I will also think about the sorrow God feels over all those who kick against the goad because they do not know him or trust him.

Prayer:

My Jesus, thank you for taking care of me by the boundaries you set. Now, how can I comfort you today for all those who say to you, "I hate you!"?

Part 10

When You Need a Miracle
Discovering the Peace that Seems Impossible

GOD'S DREAMS ARE BIGGER
Making Peace with Our Past for the Sake of a Better Future
by Kira Marie McCullough

What happens when our most cherished dreams turn to dust in our hands?

Like you, I have suffered my share of shattered dreams. But you and I are not alone. There are many broken-hearted people in the world, carrying a cross of pain because of the wounds of deferred hope. Perhaps, the greatest of all heart aches is that of broken relationships.

How do we move forward into the future with joy and expectation when we carry the memories of bruised friendships, lost loves, and broken marriages? How do we regain peace and find hope for the future?

When I am tempted to feel sadness at the recollection of my failed relationships, I find encouragement in this powerful truth:

God's Dreams are Bigger than Ours

God's dreams rise above our failures, flaws, and sins—he takes the painful endings of our lives and recreates new beginnings. Our part is to be willing and humble.

The story of Joseph in the Old Testament often overshadows the subplot featuring his father, Jacob. Not only did Jacob grieve the disappearance of his favorite son for many years, but he endured the bickering, deceitful arrogance of his remaining sons.

"Now Israel (Jacob) loved Joseph above all his sons,

because he had him in his old age; and made him a coat of divers colors. And his brethren seeing that he was loved by his father, more than all his sons, hated him, and could not speak peaceably to him."

~Genesis 37:3, 4

The brothers were furious that Joseph was their father's favorite, and so they plotted to kill him. An older, wiser brother, Ruben, suggested that they simply throw him into a well and leave him there, for he had every intention of rescuing the boy later; however, when some traders on camels came by in Ruben's absence, the others conspired to sell the boy to them, "for twenty pieces of silver, and they led him into Egypt." (Gen. 37:28)

The envious brothers dipped the boy's special robe in animal blood, took the cloak to their father Jacob, and lied to him that his son had been killed by wild beasts. Though he did not know that his sons were deceiving him, their lies wounded Jacob's heart, and his grief overwhelmed him.

Little did Jacob know that God was dreaming of restoration and peace

In the meantime, his son was on his way to Egypt, where Joseph would plummet from sonship to slavery. Yet, Joseph's sense of duty and integrity never flagged, and his master noticed.

"The Lord was with him, and he was a prosperous man in all things, and he dwelt in his master's house."

~Genesis 39:2

Also dwelling in his master's house was the wife of his master, who set her eyes upon Joseph, desiring to commit adultery. When Joseph refused her advances, she accused him of having attacked her, and when her husband heard about it, he decided to put Joseph into prison.

While there, Joseph became known as a dream interpreter. He helped many, but when they were released from jail, they forgot all about him. Then, the leader of Egypt, Pharaoh, had a troubling dream. He was told of the dream interpreter and commanded that Joseph be brought out of prison. After hearing the details of the Egyptian's dream, Joseph told Pharaoh that the vision was of a pending famine, and he counseled:

"…readiness against the famine of seven years to come, which shall oppress Egypt, that the land shall not be consumed with scarcity." This pleased the Pharaoh greatly, and he put Joseph in charge of his house and the whole land of Egypt, "…only in the kingly throne will I be above thee." (Gen. 41:40)

We may think that Joseph's promotion was the pinnacle of the story. But it was not. God had bigger dreams.

Fast forward seven years, and Pharaoh's vision had come true—there was a severe famine in the whole world, and only Egypt was prepared with storehouses of grain. In their wilderness tents, food shortages afflicted Jacob and his family, so he sent his sons (Joseph's brothers) to Egypt.

Joseph, with wisdom and cunning, used the opportunity to teach them a lesson; thus, he accused them of being spies, put them in jail for three days, and later let them go (except for Ruben) commanding them to return with their youngest brother in order to prove their identities.

He knew them, but they did not know that this tall, thirty-year old leader of Egypt—second in command to Pharaoh—was the little brother that they had thrown into the well and sold to merchants years earlier. While confined in their cells:

"…they talked to one another: We deserve to suffer these things, because we have sinned against our brother…therefore, is this affliction come upon us." (Gen. 42:21)

Here in the cold, wet prison, we overhear the brothers lamenting their sin. We see their repentance. And to think that these were the very same brothers who had so callously and without compunction cast away their younger sibling! From the pit of envy to the depths of remorse, these sons of Jacob had fallen, only to rise again in humble sorrow.

Joseph's promotion was not the penultimate moment, though it was important. God also had a plan for his brothers—not only to feed them physically, but to heal their sin-sick souls.

After releasing his brothers from prison, Joseph finally revealed himself, with many tears and much forgiveness:

> "I am Joseph, your brother, whom you sold in Egypt. Be not afraid, and let it not seem to you such a hard case that you sold me into these countries: for God sent me before you into Egypt for your preservation." He says further, "And God sent me before, that you may be preserved upon the earth and may have food to live. Not by your counsel was I sent hither but by the will of God...."
>
> ~Genesis 45:4, 5, 7, 8

After their celebration and reconciliation, Joseph sent them home with gifts, asking them to bring the entire family back to Egypt. Joseph yearned to see the rest of his family, especially his father. When the brothers returned to Canaan, they told their father that Joseph was alive, "Which when Jacob heard, he awaked as it were out of a deep sleep, yet did not believe them." (Gen. 45:26)

I understand Jacob's disbelief. When we live far too long in the barren and dry desert of unfulfilled dreams, we shut down. We stop feeling. Stop believing.

The human tendency to despair transcends all places and times. Today, you and I live in a culture that sets us up to think that it is normal to be sad, to suffer broken families, to lose our jobs, our health, and our homes. When we accept what others tell us is normal, we lose sight of the impossible. Our faith in a God of "dreams come true" dries up and blows away on the wind like autumn leaves.

Jacob did not see his beloved son, but he did see the evidence that Joseph was still alive. This was enough to renew a mustard seed of faith.

But when he saw the wagons loaded with treasures, he said, "It is enough for me, if Joseph my son be yet living; I will go and see him before I die." (Gen. 45:28)

The subplot of Jacob is a story of hope for my future and yours—Deserts of despair can be transformed by God overnight. The good news of rain comes to our ears, and we begin to awaken to the possibility that the dream we have secretly been wishing for may actually come true. I have seen this in my own life. There was a "today" when I could not see that my next "tomorrow" would bring:

- Our second child, after six years of barrenness
- The beautiful restoration of my relationship with my biological sister, after thirty years of separation
- The fulfillment of my life-long dream to write books, after years of putting the dream "on the shelf"
- The reconciliation with my father as my "best friend," after decades of a strained relationship
- Two grandsons, born from the body of my youngest daughter despite being afflicted with cystic fibrosis

God's dreams for us are so much greater than us

Notice that many of my "tomorrows" included restoration of relationships, and healing of deep desires and hopes. Not only was I blessed through these answered prayers, but so were many others.

We never dream singularly; God wants to do more than simply fulfill us. He wants to reach others with his love and forgiveness, through us. The story of Jacob, his son Joseph, and his brothers is an analogy for you and me, and the whole world. The story shouts out to us that we need not fear what we see around us, whether absence of loved ones, famine of crops or scarcity of virtues—God can turn anything bad into something good.

God's dreams extend beyond the world we live in today

There are mysterious passages in the bible that hint at something extraordinary yet to happen. From the Old Testament to the New, we read that God plans to renew the earth and bring peace to all nations. He envisions a day when all envy and lies shall cease; when the sorrow for our sins is greater than our selfish passions; the hour when we happily admit our faults and penance with joy. He promises that there is a coming time of reconciliation between husbands and wives, sisters and brothers, parents and children; a final rest for creation, when wars will cease, and strife will end. Until then, we may see "little" miracles in our lives; but a bigger miracle is coming.

However, we must be forewarned: As long as divisions continue between families, bitterness and unforgiveness brew in hearts, and the voices of political figures lie that "peace has come" while all around us we see chaos and fear—this means that the world is still in the waiting room of the Great Physician. Jesus warns us that if a "fake" doctor walks in pretending to offer the remedy for the sickness caused by lost dreams and offering peace and security—be skeptical.

Jesus answered: "Watch out that no one deceives you."
~Matthew 24:4

The truth is that only God can heal all wounds and bestow the peace that passes all understanding. Just as my childhood days concluded with the tender words of my mother, "sweet dreams," so, too shall the story of humanity close on a wondrous note, like the final melody lines of hope in the climax of a glorious symphony… and the song will ring peacefully for many generations.

For God has pledged that one day his kingdom will rule in all hearts that hunger for him, and that the knowledge of the Lord will cover the earth as the waters cover the sea.

Storing Up Treasures in Heaven

Are there dreams that you have abandoned? Relationships that seem irreparable? Hopes that have disappeared?

Resist the temptation to wallow in sadness! Instead, ask God to replace your grief with joy, your hopelessness with hope, your lack of enthusiasm with the fullness of his Holy Spirit.

Remember that the Holy Spirit has been give to you to help you regain your balance and keep moving forward into the good things God has for your life. Ask the Heavenly Father to pour out grace into the deepest places of your heart, through the Holy Spirit. God longs to give this gift!

> *Now suppose one of you fathers is asked by his son for a fish; he will not give him a snake instead of a fish, will he? Or if he is asked for an egg, he will not give him a scorpion, will he? If you then, being evil, know how to give good gifts to your children, how much more will your heavenly Father give the Holy Spirit to those who ask Him?*
>
> ~Luke 11:11–13

Meditate on this truth

God can take your unfortunate circumstances and turn them into new blessings. Your "ending" may really be a new beginning, because God has bigger dreams that he wants to share with you!

Throughout the week, memorize these scripture verses:

Now may the God of hope fill you with all joy and peace

in believing, so that you will abound in hope by the power of the Holy Spirit.

~Romans 15:13

'For I know the plans that I have for you,' declares the LORD, 'plans for welfare and not for calamity to give you a future and a hope.

'Then you will call upon Me and come and pray to Me, and I will listen to you.

'You will seek Me and find Me when you search for Me with all your heart.

~Jeremiah 29:11–13

THE HIGHEST MOUNTAIN
Peace at Last

by Keb Burns

So, after all this wonderful advice, you might be thinking that my life is an oasis of tranquility in this troubled world. No, I'm just like you. I am always trying, failing, and starting over. Though my overall trajectory over the years has been upwards (more or less), I have not yet made it to the summit of this mountain called Peace.

Many of you are staring up at the same peak, wondering if you can ever climb it. In fact, there are so many people struggling to get there, a huge, multi-million-dollar industry of self-help books, videos, conferences, and motivational speakers has grown up around the base of this mountain like the hundreds of tents that are scattered around the base of Mt. Everest during climbing season. Self-help gimmicks won't do you any good. You won't summit without the Ultimate Sherpa. You can only get to the top with God's help.

So, what will you find when you get to the top of this mountain called Peace? Believe it or not, you will find a tree growing in the middle of a golden city. The Apostle John was given a vision of it.

He took me in spirit to a great, high mountain and showed me the holy city Jerusalem coming down out of heaven from God. It gleamed with the splendor of God. Its radiance was like that of a precious stone, like jasper, clear as crystal... The twelve gates were twelve pearls, each of the gates made from a single pearl; and the street of the city was of pure gold, transparent as glass... Then the angel showed me the river of life-giving water, sparkling like crystal, flowing from the throne of God and of the Lamb down the middle of its street. On either side of the river grew the tree of life that produces fruit twelve times a year, once each month; the leaves of the trees serve as medicine for the nations... I heard a loud voice from the throne saying, "Behold, God's dwelling is with the human race. He will dwell with them and they will be his people and God himself will always be with them [as their God]. He will wipe every tear from their eyes, and there shall be no more death or mourning, wailing or pain, [for] the old order has passed away."

~Revelation 21 & 22, various verses

God will wipe away every tear from our eyes. This is the pinnacle of peace and joy. But what is this tree that grows in the City of God? We've seen this tree before in the first book of Genesis. And we see it again now, in the last book, Revelation. In both books, it symbolically represents Eternal Life. It means we were given Eternal Life at the beginning of time, but because we lost it, we don't see the tree again in Scripture until the last book. The Tree is fully restored to us at the end of the world. But did you notice the Tree isn't growing in the same place each time?

In Genesis, the Tree of Life grows in the home of Adam and Eve, in Eden, a world of beauty, order, plenty, and peace. It is a beautiful garden with plants and animals and trees. God came and visited there in their home, walking and talking with them in the cool of the evening. This is a description of a place of perfect natural happiness.

At the end of the Bible, the Tree of Life is no longer in the Garden of Eden. It now grows in a city of gold bedecked with jewels and illuminated with the light of God's own presence. God doesn't just visit there, he lives there. And we are invited to live there, too, in his home. This isn't a place of natural happiness like the Garden of Eden, it's a place of supernatural happiness. This tells us that God didn't just redeem us, he elevated us to an even higher state than we had before we fell from grace.

Why does the city come down out of Heaven to rest on the mountaintop? What does this mean? It suggests that when we climb the mountain to reach God, he graciously responds by coming down to meet us. This mountain symbolism can be found in other parts of Scripture, as well. For example, Abraham climbs up into the mountains to find God, as do Moses and Elijah, and God comes down to meet them on the mountain.

But it means more than that. The image of heaven coming down to earth is an image of the Lord's Prayer, "thy will be done, on earth as it is in Heaven." In this vision, God expresses his most ardent desire: that everything on earth be as good, true, and beautiful as it is in Heaven. God's Will comes down from Heaven and touches the earth. We climb the mountain to find God's Will.

Doing God's Will on earth as it is done in Heaven sounds daunting, but if Jesus asked us to pray for it, it must be possible. With practice and God's grace, we can at least learn how to bring God's perfect Will down onto our little patch of earth, one day at a time. Let's keep this simple. As you go through the day, pause now and then and silently ask yourself:

- ∾ Am I doing the right thing right now?
- ∾ Is this the right time, place, and circumstance to be doing it?
- ∾ Am I doing it for the right reason?

If you can say yes to all three questions, you are doing the Will of God today. If you can't, well, welcome to the human race. Adjust accordingly and persevere.

I said earlier that the Tree of Life appears only twice in the Bible. To be precise, it appears only twice in its full glory. It does make an appearance one more time, but in a terrible disguise. We see it on another mountain, Mount Calvary. It is the tree on which our Savior was crucified. It may not look as beautiful as it was in the Garden of Eden or as it is in the city of gold, but make no mistake, it is the same Tree of Eternal Life from which the river of grace flows and leaves heal the nations. At the foot of this tree, the Cross of Jesus, you will find all the strength and wisdom you need to follow the Will of God.

Storing Up Treasures in Heaven

Looking Within:
    As I come to the end of my thirty days of reflections on peace, I resolve to continue to build peace in my life and the lives of those around me. Every time I say the Lord's Prayer, I will silently add "…Thy will be done *in me*, on earth as it is in heaven…"

Prayer:
    My Jesus, I long to be with you forever in the bejeweled City of Gold, the Heavenly Jerusalem. Grant me every grace I need to continue climbing the mountain of the Lord, step by step, day by day. I know you are not waiting for me at the top, you are walking by my side, climbing the mountain with me as you once climbed Calvary. Never let me take my eyes off of you until we reach the end of this journey together.

ACKNOWLEDGEMENTS

We are thankful for the editing support of Mike Coyne, who helped us in the early phases of writing this book. We are also grateful for our dear friends, Dina Cavazos and Tina Marsh, who spent countless hours workshopping these pieces in our writers' group.

And we are thankful to you, dear readers. Without you, who would we tell our stories to? Could we ask you a big favor? If you've enjoyed *Treasures of Grace: The Gift of Peace*, would you consider telling a friend and maybe writing a review on your favorite book seller's website? We want as many people as possible to discover our stories and word of mouth is still the best advertising! Tell a friend and write a review. We will be eternally grateful.

Follow the *Treasures of Grace* Facebook Page:

@TreasuresofGrace

KIRA MARIE MCCULLOUGH

Kira Marie McCullough is a mother, grandmother, and writer who see her life as an imperfect journey towards truth, beauty, and goodness. Through her writing, she seeks to glorify God and bless others, creating works of eloquence, excellence, and artistry for generations to enjoy and cherish. She debuted *King of the Lake and Other Stories* with WordCrafts Press in 2022. These nine unique short stories run the gamut of genres, from the woeful love story of a family's healing after being broken by divorce in "King of the Lake," to a couple's ironic TV obsession that sweeps them into a storm of biblical proportions, in "Too Much TV, You'll Go Blind." She is currently working on a book of historical fiction set in a farming community in Kansas, which takes the reader through the hardships, love stories, and faith of its people.

Follow KMM's writerly journey on Facebook:
https://www.facebook.com/kiramarie.mccullough/
Enjoy her daily peaceful inspirations on the Facebook Page:
@SomePeace&Coffee

KEB BURNS

Keb Burns is a Texas author, artist, and gardener who uses her pen and brush to call attention to God's presence in ordinary life. Her work invites the observer away from the chaos of the world into the quiet glen of contemplation. Drawing on 40 years' experience teaching religion and a career in commercial art and landscape design, she strives to make difficult concepts easy to understand, and invisible realities almost visible. She finds her deepest joy in nature, where the filmy veil that cloaks the face of the Creator is the thinnest.

Follow Keb on her Substack "Fair Wind, Sailing West"
kebburns.substack.com

Also Available From
WORDCRAFTS PRESS

Learning as I Go
by Christy Bass Adams

In the Boat with Jesus
by Marian Rizzo

God in the Commonplace
by Beverly Clopton

Illuminations
by Paula K. Parker

When the Other Boot Drops
by Jeff Keene II

www.wordcrafts.net

www.ingramcontent.com/pod-product-compliance
Lightning Source LLC
Chambersburg PA
CBHW021632120626
46545CB00002B/512